SUCCEED IN MATHS

STRUCTURED MATHEMATICS

FOR

THE NATIONAL CURRICULUM

KEYSTAGE TWO
with an introduction to Keystage Three

Mike Bell and John Elston

ORIFLAMME PUBLISHING
London

SUCCEED IN MATHS

by **Mike Bell** and **John Elston**

© **Oriflamme Publishing Ltd. 1997**

ISBN   0 948093 17 X

First Edition 1997

Oriflamme Publishing Ltd.
60 Charteris Road
London N4 3AB

Phototypeset in 12 on 13 point Times New Roman.
Printed and bound in the British Isles by
The Guernsey Press Co. Ltd., Guernsey, Channel Islands.

SUCCEED IN MATHS

Introduction

Succeed in Maths presents the necessary mathematical skills and knowledge for Keystage Two (leading on to Keystage Three) of the National Curriculum. The teaching is presented by subject topic, and is supported by practice exercises in each topic, with revision exercises and check tests at the end.

For primary schools the book can be used in the top classes as preparation for the transition to secondary school. It is particularly useful in preparing pupils for the entry examinations to independent, grammar and public schools. It is designed to provide stimulation and practice for children who have ability in the subject, as well as giving all the necessary basic skills.

For secondary schools, the book is suitable as the basis for an introductory teaching scheme, reinforcing primary school studies and carrying them through to secondary level. It is intended to take children smoothly through the transition from Keystage Two to Keystage Three.

Succeed in Maths is particularly suitable for use by children and parents at home. The text is presented so that children can work through each topic area by themselves, with parental or other adult support. The methods use conform with current mathematical practice. Parents will find the book easy to use with their children, and will have the answer to "We don't do it that way now !" at their fingertips. Very detailed examples are used throughout, with every stage of the working explained. Even adults who wish to brush up their maths may well find the book a great help.

In the classroom, teachers will be able to use the topic structure and the subdivisions as a basis for their own lesson plans. The practice exercises with each topic can be used in a variety of ways, and may be readily adapted and expanded as the teacher sees fit. Practical work can be readily adapted from the examples used in the book. The tests have been set out formally as a preparation for examinations, but they may also be used as illustrative examples, and worked through with the class, in groups or individually.

For all users *Succeed in Maths* is intended to provide a permanent source of reference, easy to consult and use, and very convenient as a tool for revision.

The authors, Mike Bell and John Elston, of Warwick School, have over fifty years of classroom teaching experience between them. They have used their own practical experience to develop the methods used in the book, and all the topics are presented in ways that have proved successful over the years. All of the material has been tried in the classroom.

Succeed in Maths is based on a belief in the crucial importance of learning the basic skills and knowledge in maths. Without these sure foundations, subsequent efforts will not achieve the results. The aim of the book is that its users should achieve success in mathematics; that they should both possess the basic skills and understand them; and that they should gain good passes in all the examinations in maths - one of the most vital of all subjects - which they will take.

TABLE of CONTENTS

Other Educational Titles

SUCCEED IN MATHS - ANSWERS *(Answers to all exercises & tests in the present volume)*
by Mike Bell and John Elston 32 pp paperback ISBN 0 948093 18 8   £2.75

The Rules of Maths by John Connor & Pat Soper 80 pp paperback   ISBN 0 948093 06 4   £5.25
A handbook setting out the core of mathematical knowledge needed by all children (and adults). The foundations of primary and secondary school mathematics are laid out in a simple and straightforward format. Each topic has a separate chapter, in which it is fully and explained with worked examples. The text is especially suitable for children in the nine to thirteen age range, and covers both traditional and modern mathematics. It provides an ideal learning source and reference book for children, parents and teachers
Modular Maths   by John Connor & Pat Soper 80 pp paperback   ISBN 0 948093 07 2   £4.95
A book of exercises covering all the elements required for mathematics up to the middle years of secondary school and beyond. Suitable for use as a maths foundation course in conjunction with *Rules of Maths*, and as a convenient book of examples and problems for practice at home or in school. The questions are set out in 38 double-page modules, each of which has three sections.
Maths Answers Booklet   15 pp paper   ISBN 0 948093 09 9   £2.00
Covers all the questions in *Modular Maths*, together with the trial examples and tests in *Rules of Maths*.

The Rules of English by Edward Marsh M.A. (Oxon.)   128 pp paperback ISBN 0 948093 15 3 £5.50
A full summary of all the rules of correct English usage, written in a clear, straightforward and logical manner. It covers all the essential material for the curriculum from junior school to school leaving age, and is suitable for children from 9 to 18. It can be used as a textbook, with the pupil beginning at the first rule and working through the book to the end. It is also suitable for exam revision, as a convenient handbook for ready reference, or as a study book for those whose first language is not English.

The **Help Yourself to English** series by Edward Marsh M.A. (Oxon.)

This consists of *The Rules of English* together with an additional set of five books which cover all the essential basics of the language in greater detail. These five books are laid out as a page of information (Factsheet) facing a page of exercises (Worksheet) on each topic. They combine traditional content with a sensible and interesting approach, and are designed for easy use at home or school. They provide all the essentials of writing and understanding English, together with the necessary skills for written examinations in English language, including Common Entrance, the national tests at 11+ and 14+, and even GCSE.
Book One : Words   64 pp paperback ISBN 0 948093 01 3 £3.95
Book Two : Sentences   48 pp paperback ISBN 0 948093 02 1 £3.50
Basic grammar in *Book One*, leading onto the construction and structure of sentences in *Book Two*.
Book Three : Composition   64 pp paperback ISBN 0 948093 03 X £4.25
Book Four : Comprehension   48 pp paperback ISBN 0 948093 04 8 £3.50
Essay and composition skills broken down and explained in detail, and the technique of doing comprehension exercises fully explained through examples, hints and advice.
Book Five : Spelling   80 pp paperback ISBN 0 948093 05 6 £4.25
English spelling explained on phonetic principles, working up from simple words to problem spellings.
Answers Booklets (covering all the questions set in the books of the *Help Yourself to English* series).
Book One: Words - Answers   14 pp paper ISBN 0 948093 10 2 £1.50
Book Two: Sentences - Answers   22 pp paper ISBN 0 948093 11 0 £2.50
Book Three: Composition - Answers   18 pp paper ISBN 0 948093 12 9 £2.00
Book Four: Comprehension - Answers   10 pp paper ISBN 0 948093 13 7 £1.00
Book Five: Spelling - Answers   10 pp paper ISBN 0 948093 14 5 £1.00
The Rules of English - Answers   16 pp paper ISBN 0 948093 16 1 £2.00

Available from good book shops, or directly from: Grantham Book Services Ltd., Isaac Newton Way, Alma Park Industrial Estate, Grantham, Lincs NG31 9SD (Fax : 01476 567314. Tel: 01476 567421).

Oriflamme Publishing, 60 Charteris Road, London N4 3AB

WHOLE NUMBERS AND PLACE VALUE

Our number system is called **The Decimal System**. It is based on the number **10**.

As soon as we have ten *units* we carry one into the tens place.
As soon as we have ten *tens*, we carry one into the hundreds place, and so on.

So as the digits move ONE PLACE TO THE **LEFT** they become 10 TIMES **BIGGER.**
As they move TWO PLACES TO THE LEFT, they become 100 TIMES BIGGER, and so on.

As the digits move ONE PLACE TO THE **RIGHT**, they become 10 TIMES **SMALLER.**
As they move TWO PLACES TO THE RIGHT, they become 100 TIMES SMALLER, and so on.

Look at this number, where each of the digits has been marked with a letter:

Three thousand, three hundred and thirty three: 3 3 3 3
                                                       a b c d

We can answer some questions about it:

Question:	How many times bigger than **c** is **b** ?
Answer:	*TEN times bigger, because to get from c to b we move **one** place to the **left**.*
Question:	How many times is **b** bigger than **d** ?
Answer:	*ONE HUNDRED times bigger, because to get from b to a, we move **two** places left.*
Question:	How many times is **a** smaller than **b** ?
Answer:	*TEN times smaller, because to get from a to b, we move **one** place to the **right**.*
Question:	How many times smaller than **a** is **d** ?
Answer:	*ONE THOUSAND times smaller, because to get from b to d, we move **three** places **right**.*

Exercise 1

Look at this number, where each of the digits has been marked with a letter: 4 4 4 4 4
                                                                                    a b c d e

Now answer the questions and *give your reasons* for each answer.

1. Which is greater, **c** or **e** ?
2. Is **d** smaller than **a** ?   If so by how many times ?
3. Which is greater, **a** or **b** ? By how many times is one greater than the other ?
4. How many times smaller than **b** is **e** ?
5. How many times is **a** greater than **c** ?
6. Make up a question of your own, using the number 44 444
7. Using a number of your own, make up some more questions. Answer them, and then get your
    teacher or your parents to check the answers.

Here are the most important number values for you to learn:

	Millions	Hundred Thousands	Ten Thousands	Thousands	Hundreds	Tens	Units
(a)	2	6	3	2	5	1	3
(b)	5	0	1	1	2	0	6

We always read numbers from the **left to right**.

So number (a) reads:
     two million, six hundred and thirty-two thousand, five hundred and thirteen
And number (b) reads:
     five million, eleven thousand, two hundred and six.

When we write numbers in digits, it is usual to leave a slight gap between the millions and hundred thousands, and also between the thousands and the hundreds. Another way of doing this is with a comma.

So number (a) would be recorded as: 2 632 513 and number (b) as: 5 011 206

When reading numbers involving thousands, we total how many thousands we have altogether.

For example:	100 Th	10 Th	Th	H	T	U
(c)	2	1	6	7	1	9
(d)		6	1	2	8	9

Number (c) reads: Two hundred and sixteen thousand, seven hundred and nineteen.
Number (d) reads: Sixty-one thousand, two hundred and eighty-nine.

Is this how we would write in columns the number: ' forty-two thousand and fifty' ?

10Th.	Th.	H	T	U
	42		5	0

No, this would be wrong. Notice how the 42 has been written in the thousands column. But as we count in tens we really have four groups of ten thousand. These should therefore be written in the ten thousands column. So the number should correctly be written like this:

10Th.	Th.	H	T	U
4	2	0	5	0

(Notice how we must put a zero in any empty columns, such as the hundreds in this example.)

2

The same principle also applies to even larger numbers.

So *three hundred and eleven thousand four hundred and nine* should be written like this:

100Th.	10Th.	Th.	H	T	U
3	1	1	4	0	9

and **NOT** like this:

100Th.	10Th.	Th.	H	T	U
		311	4		9

Exercise 1A

Write these numbers in figures:

1. seven hundred and sixty-three
2. four thousand six hundred and seventy-three
3. sixty thousand, five hundred and nineteen
4. eighteen thousand and four
5. fifty thousand five hundred and forty-two.
6. nine hundred and ninety thousand and ninety-one
7. four hundred and eleven thousand two hundred and six
8. three hundred and forty thousand, nine hundred and eleven
9. thirty-six million, one hundred and eight thousand and fifty nine.
10. four hundred and seventy million, two hundred and one thousand, one hundred and eighty.

Exercise 1B

Write these numbers in words:

1. 28 174
2. 439 207
3. 992 254
4. 1 236 191
5. 502 502
6. 1 306 600
7. 600 540
8. 11 432 789
9. 99 222 234
10. 812 125 156

Always remember that we count in groups of ten.

The number sixty-three is made up of six tens. Each ten is worth ten units. And there are also another three units. So altogether there are 63 units.

Look at these examples:

(a)

H	T	U
1	7	1

There are several ways of describing this number.

In this number we have one hundred, seven tens and one unit.
We could also say we have seventeen tens and one unit.
We could also say we have 171 units.

(b)   How many tens altogether and units altogether are there in the number: 473 ?

There are forty-seven tens altogether.
And there are four hundred and seventy-three units altogether.

(c)   In the number 3 064 we have:

------------ thousands altogether,
------------ hundreds altogether,
------------ tens altogether,
and ------------ units altogether.

Can you fill in the blanks correctly ? The answer is at the bottom of the page.

Try these other practical examples (answers at the bottom of the page) :

(d)   603 715

------------ hundred thousands altogether, ------------ ten thousands altogether, ------------ thousands altogether, ------------ hundreds altogether, ------------ tens altogether, ------------ units altogether.

(e)   315 206 095

------------ hundred millions altogether, ------------ ten millions altogether, ------------ millions altogether, ------------ hundred thousands altogether, ------------ ten thousands altogether, ------------ thousands altogether, ------------ hundreds altogether, ------------ tens altogether, ------------ units altogether.

Exercise 2

1.   How many tens altogether are there in 647 ?
2.   How many units are there altogether in 4 625 ?
3.   How many thousands are there altogether in 52 715 ?
4.   How many millions are there altogether in 637 207 459 ?
5.   How many hundreds are there altogether in 312 689 ?
6.   How many tens of thousands are there altogether in 8 176 259 ?
7.   How many tens of millions are there altogether in 849 602 713 ?
8.   How many hundreds are there altogether in 8 761 203 ?
9.   How many thousands are there altogether in 7 568 973 ?
10.   How many tens are there altogether in 3 010 715 ?

Answers to the practical examples only:

(c):   3 thousands; 30 hundreds; 306 tens; and 3 064 units.
(d):   (in order) - 6; 60; 603; 6 037; 60 371; 603 715.
(e)   (in order) - 3; 31; 315; 3 152; 31 520; 315 206; 3 152 060; 31 520 609; 315 206 095.

ROUNDING OFF

The correct word for this is *approximating* to the nearest amount.

Look at these examples:

What would these numbers be rounded off (approximated) to the nearest *ten* ?

(a)   68   (b)   71   (c)   136.

Answers:

(a)   70   (b)   70   (c)   140.

How do we get to these answers ?   This is the procedure:

(1)   First look at the column we are approximating to. In these examples it is the tens column.
We shall take number (c) first. The tens column in this number has a three in it.

(2)   We mark or highlight the column: 1 **3** 6

(3)   Look at the digit to the RIGHT of the highlighted digit. In this case it is a 6

If the digit to the right is 5 OR MORE, we increase the column we are rounding off by one.

If the digit to the right is LESS THAN 5, we do not change the column we are rounding off.

In this case, the highlighted digit is 3, and the digit to the right is 5 or more (6).
So the 3 becomes four.

(4)   The digit to the right of that column becomes zero.
So the 6 becomes a zero, and we are left with: 140

Once we have rounded off, ALL the remaining figures to the right of the column become ZEROS.
Even if there are twenty columns of figures to the right - they all become zeros.

We can see what happens where the number to the right of the highlighted column is less than five,
in the case of number (b) - 71:

The highlighted digit is the 7 in the tens column: **7**1
The digit to the right of it is 1. This is less than 5, so the 7 stays the same. The 1 becomes zero.
So 71 rounded off to the nearest ten is 70

It is important to remember, whether you are rounding a number up or down, that the digits to the right
of the column you are approximating to, must all become zeros.
Never change any of the digits to the *left* of the column.

5

Here are two more examples:

(d)   Approximate 7 341 to the nearest hundred.

    (1)   We are looking at the hundreds column this time, and the digit there is: 3
    (2)   We highlight the column: 7 **3**41
    (3)   Look at the digit to the right of the highlighted one.
           It is a 4. It is less than five, so we do NOT increase the highlighted digit.
    (4)   All the figures to the right of the highlighted column become zeros.

So 7341 to the nearest hundred is 7 300

(e)   Round off 42 892 to the nearest thousand.

    (1)   Check the thousands column. The digit is: 2
    (2)   Highlight the column: 4**2** 892
    (3)   Look at the digit to the right.
           It is an 8. This is five or more, so we DO increase the highlighted digit.
           The 2 in the thousands column therefore become a 3.
    (4)   All the figures to the right become zeros.

So 42 892 to the nearest thousand is 43 000

Exercise 3

(1)   Round off to the nearest ten: (a) 89   (b) 73   (c) 131
(2)   Round off to the nearest hundred: (a) 314   (b) 789   (c) 1 466
(3)   Approximate to the nearest thousand: (a) 8 376 (b) 21 336 (c) 817 968
(4)   Approximate to the nearest ten thousand: (a) 47 819 (b) 203 364 (c) 7 146 897
(5)   Round off to the nearest hundred thousand:
              (a) 764 813   (b) 2 133 218   (c) 617 289 714
(6)   Approximate to the nearest million:
              (a) 6 974 613   (b) 10 140 283   (c) 897 687 403

Exercise 4   Revision of Numbers Topics

Write the following numbers in digits:

(1)   eight hundred and seventy-four   (2)   fifteen thousand eight hundred and thirty
(3)   seven million, six hundred and thirty-eight thousand, nine hundred and seventy-five
(4)   eighty million eight hundred thousand eight hundred and eighty
(5)   one hundred million five hundred and four thousand nine hundred and seventy-eight

Write the following numbers in words:

(6)   39   (7)   4 603   (8)   345 000
(9)   11 010 003   (10)   99 420 359

THE FOUR RULES OF NUMBER

ADDITION

It is very important when adding numbers to keep the digits in their correct columns. Make sure that the units of each number being added are all in the units column, and the tens all in the tens column, and the hundreds all in the hundreds column, and so on.

There are several different words which tell us to add:

(a)   Find the sum of   (b)   Add together   (c)   Find the total of
(d)   Increase by   (e)   Find the aggregate of .... and ....
(f)   Which number is .... greater than ....

The following example sets out an addition sum with several numbers. Make sure that your addition sums are set out this way, with the correct digits under each other in the correct column.
Write the figures you carry as small numbers under the answer, and do not forget to add them together with the numbers in the column.

Example 1 - Addition

Finds the sum of: 2 956,   33 207,   1 234 567,   16,   and 26 041.

```
          2    9 5 6
         3 3   2 0 7
    1   2 3 4  5 6 7
                1 6
  +      2 6   0 4 1
  _____
    1   2 9 6  7 8 7
  _____
         1  1   1  2
```

Add up each column in turn.

If the answer is more than ten, carry the tens and put the units in the answer space.

Then add up the next column.

Do not forget to add the number carried.

Work through the example carefully, and make sure you know how to do this sort of simple sum.

SUBTRACTION

As for addition, you must make sure that the correct digits go in the correct columns. A subtraction sum can only be done with two numbers at a time.

Make sure that you always subtract the smaller number from the larger number.

So the *smaller* number must go *underneath* the larger one.

There are several different words which tell us to subtract:

(a)   Take away   (b)   Find the number which is .... less than ....
(c)   Decrease by   (d)   Reduce by   (e)   Minus
(f)   Find the difference between .... and ....   (g)   Subtract

The following example sets out a subtraction sum. Make sure that your subtraction sums are set out this way, with the correct digits under each other in the correct column, and the smaller number on the bottom line of the sum.

Example 2 - Subtraction

Find the difference between 87 654 and 98 765

```
    9 8    7 6 5
-   8 7    6 5 4
  _____
    1 1    1 1 1
  _____
```

Example 2a - Subtraction with borrowing

Decrease 3 276 by 1 885

```
    3    2 7 6
-   1    8 8 5
  _____

  _____
```

It is not always possible to subtract each separate digit of the bottom number from the corresponding digit of the top number, because the bottom digit may be bigger.

In this example the lower digit is larger than the upper digit in both the tens column and also in the hundreds column. Look at the working on the following page which uses the example to show how this problem can be solved.

$$
\begin{array}{ccccc}
 & ^{2}3 & ^{11}2 & ^{1}7 & 6 \\
- & 1 & 8 & 8 & 5 \\
\hline
 & 1 & 3 & 9 & 1 \\
\hline
\end{array}
$$

1. Subtract the units: 6 - 5 = 1.   Write the 1 in the answer.

2. Now deal with the tens column: 7 - 8 is impossible.
    So we borrow 1 from the hundreds column. (This is one hundred, so it is worth 10 tens.)
    We add it to the digit on the top line of the tens column, which now becomes: 17 tens
    At the same time we must reduce the hundreds column by the one we have borrowed.
    So the 2 in the hundreds column is reduced to 1.

3. Now we can subtract the tens: 17 - 8 = 9

4. Next deal with the hundreds column: 1 - 8 is impossible.
    So we borrow one from the thousands column. (This is one thousand, so it is worth 10 hundreds.)
    We add it to the digit on the top line of the hundreds column. This digit was originally 2, but we
    have already reduced it to 1. So now it becomes: 11 hundreds.
    At the same time we must reduce the thousands column by the one we have borrowed.
    So the 3 in the thousands column is reduced to 2.

5. Now we can subtract the hundreds: 11 - 8 = 3

6. Subtract the thousands column (where we have reduced the 3 to 2): 2 - 1 = 1

Notice how we write the figures we borrow and also figures we have reduced as small digits above.

Work through the example carefully, and make sure you know how to do this sort of subtraction.

Exercise 5

1.   987 + 463
2.   9 765 - 5 312
3.   89 999 + 65 231
4.   Increase 2 543 275 by 55 293
5.   Carry out this addition: 7 + 77 + 777 + 7 777
6.   Decrease six hundred and seventy thousand by thirteen thousand four hundred and ninety-two.
7.   Find the difference between 62 801 and 203 448.
8.   What number is seventy thousand and five greater than eight hundred and seventy-seven ?
9.   Which number is 23 709 less than 123 818 ?
10. Subtract 12 962 from the sum of 9 996 and 654 112.
11. Find the aggregate of: 1 035 711, 925 700 and 80 696, and then calculate what number is
     one million two hundred and thirty thousand four hundred and nineteen less than your result.
12. Reduce 16 743 201 by 9 743 202, then increase your answer by the sum of 123 456 and 79 821.

MULTIPLICATION

Multiplication is a quick method of adding several numbers that are the same. It is impossible to multiply quickly and accurately unless you know your tables at least up to the 10x table. If you are not sure of your tables you should learn them immediately.

There are various words which mean multiply:

(a)   Times   (b)   Find the product of ....(c)   Of   (For example: 7 of 32)
(d)   Brackets are also used to mean multiplication. (For example: 9 (932) means 9 times 932.)

You will have noticed that in addition and subtraction we always begin with the units column (on the right) and work through the columns towards the left. This rule also applies to multiplication.

There are two kinds of multiplication: short multiplication and long multiplication. In both forms the multiplication sum must be set out vertically in columns. Always multiply units first, and always work from right to left.

Short Multiplication

Example 3

Find the product of 262 and 7.

```
      2    6    2
      x         7
    _____
  1   8    3    4
    _____
        4    1
```

As in addition, when the result of any one multiplication is more than 9, the units digit goes in the answer space, and the tens digit is carried. Write the carried digits rather smaller under the answer line. Make sure they are under the correct column. Do not forget to add them to the result of the next column's multiplication.

Long Multiplication

This is also known as extended multiplication. The way to do it is to carry out separate multiplication sums
for each of the digits you are multiplying by.

First you multiply by the units digit. Then you multiply by the tens digit.

But before multiplying by the tens digit, you must put a zero (0) in that line of the answer, and write your result to the left of the zero. Continue for hundreds (two zeros), thousands (three zeros) and so on.

Then add up the separate lines of the multiplications, and the result is the answer to the sum.

Example 3a

Multiply 825 by 37

```
              8   2   5
      x           3   7
    _____
      5   7   7   5
      1   1   3
    2 4   7   5   0      <<<< Notice the zero inserted when multiplying by the tens.
    2         1
    _____
    3 0   5   2   5
    _____
    1     1       1
```

The first result: 5 775 is the result of multiplying 825 by 7.
The second result: 24 750 is the result of multiplying 825 by 3 tens.

By adding the two results together we obtain the answer to the whole sum.

When you are doing this sort of multiplication you must be particularly careful not to confuse the carrying figures with the results which you are adding up. Write your carrying figures very small.

Work through this example carefully, and make sure you understand how to do this kind of sum.

Exercise 6

Set out the following multiplication sums correctly, and then work them out.

1. 264 x 7   2. 589 x 8   3. 878 x 9   4. 907 x 6
5. 737 x 29   6. 863 x 65   7. 432 x 56   8. 685 x 1395
9. What is the product of 237 and 1 420 ?   10. 11 (397)
11. Multiply one thousand and eighteen by seventy-two.   12. 9 307 x 492

DIVISION

Division is a short form of subtraction (where the same number has to be taken away many times).

There are several words which can be used for division:

(a) Share by   (b) Which number is divisible by......... ?   (c) Divide
(d) How many times will .... <u>go into</u> .... ?

Division can also be shown by writing the number to be divided (the dividend), over the top of the number it is divided by (the divisor), like this:

$$\frac{4\ 392}{9}$$

When you do division you always divide into the highest value digit first. So you start with the left hand column. This is the opposite of the method for addition, subtraction and multiplication.

After you have completed the division for the first (highest) digit, you carry any remainder to the next digit. Then you carry out the division for that digit and so on till you get to the last digit.

If there is a remainder at the end of the sum, you write it as a remainder after the answer.

You do your working out for division sums underneath, and you fill in the answer over the top.

There are two sorts of division sum: short division, and long division.

Short Division

Example 4

765 ÷ 5

Firstly the sum must be set out in the way we set out all division sums.

$$5 \,)\, \overline{7\ 6\ 5}$$

Then we divide into each digit in turn, carrying the remainder as a small digit written above the next digit (in the same way we did when writing the number borrowed in long multiplication).

$$5 \,)\, \overline{\begin{matrix} 1\ 5\ 3 \\ 7\ ^26\ ^15 \end{matrix}}$$

Example 4a (Short division with a remainder)

5 854 ÷ 7

$$7 \,)\, \overline{\begin{matrix} 8\ 3\ 6 \quad\text{r. } 2 \\ 5\ ^58\ ^25\ ^44 \end{matrix}}$$

Notice that when we start the sum we cannot divide 5 by 7, so we carry the 5 over to the eight.
We now have 58, which can be divided 7.
(We may put a zero in the answer over the 5 if wished, to make sure the digits are always put in the correct columns.)

When the final digit is reached, we have 44 (the original 4, and the 4 tens we have carried back.
The division now is: 44 ÷ 7.   6 x 7 = 42.
So there are 2 left over. This is called the remainder, and is written as r. 2.

Exercise 7

1. $4\,794 \div 6$ 2. $1\,638 \div 7$ 3. $5\,416 \div 8$ 4. $4\,466 \div 7$

5. $4\,344 \div 6$ 6. $2\,520 \div 6$ 7. $2\,744 \div 7$ 8. $3\,390 \div 5$

Long Division

Example 4b

$9\,555 \div 35$

```
                    2   7   3
          _____
    3   5 ) 9   5   5   5
          - 7   0   ↓   ↓
          _____
              2   5   5   ↓
            - 2   4   5   ↓
            _____
                  1   0   5
                - 1   0   5
                _____
                          0
```

Working out may be shown at the side of the sum, like this:

$35 \times 3 = 105$ $35 \times 2 = 70$
$35 \times 6 = 210$ $35 \times 7 = 245$

We begin as before, and since we cannot divide 35 into 9, we try to divide 35 into 95.

With long division we do not use the method of carrying numbers, we look at the two digits together: here we have a nine followed by a five, so we are dealing with 95.

However, we do not know exactly how many times 35 may go into 95, so we have to use trial and error.

Firstly we guess roughly how many times it might divide, and then we try out our guess with a few quick multiplication sums:

   35   35
  x 3   x 2
  105   ⇐ Too many.   70   ⇐ Below 95, so YES.

The 2 goes in the answer space, above the hundreds column. The seventy is subtracted from 95 (the number currently being divided).

The next number to be divided is 5 (in the tens column). This is brought down next to the 25.
So now we have 255. We repeat the procedure, dividing 35 into 255. We fill in the answer: seven.

Seven x 35 = 245. So again we perform the subtraction. There is ten left, and we bring down the remaining digit (the five). We now have 105, and we complete the division: $105 \div 35 = 3$.

Remember that not every division sum (long or short division) will work out exactly, and you must always show anything left at the end as the remainder.

Also remember that you can only successfully do division sums if you have a thorough knowledge of the multiplication tables.

Exercise 7 A

Set out the following questions correctly, and work them out by long division.

1.	$782 \div 23$	2.	$828 \div 36$	3.	$4\,056 \div 13$	4.	$5\,947 \div 19$
5.	$5\,151 \div 17$	6.	$11\,826 \div 18$	7.	$5\,555 \div 28$	8.	$7\,360 \div 43$

The following exercise provides a set of problems associated with the four rules of number. When doing it, work out what particular rule or rules you need you use, and then set out the sums involved in the correct way. Be sure to work neatly, and to show all your working out.

Exercise 8 (For: A.T.2, Levels 4 & 5)

1. The population of Bartown is 22 678, and the population of Clingsville is 32 781. If 2 467 people leave Clingsville and go to live in Bartown, what will then be the population of each town ?

2. When 33 678 and another number are added together, the answer is: 401 622. What is the other number ?

3. Thirty-one buses, each with fifty-three seats carried the supporters of Clingsville Rovers F.C. to a match. All the buses were full except the last one, which had nine empty seats. How many Clingsville supporters travelled to the match ?

4. 6 541 people watched a basketball match. 3 178 of them were men. 297 of them were boys. 176 of them were girls. The rest were women. How many women watched the match ?

5. In a theatre there are 89 rows of seats, with 29 seats in each row. How many seats altogether are there in the theatre ?

6. Four hundred and forty-six bottles of milk were delivered to a school. Each class had 31 bottles.
   (a) How many classes were there in the school ?
   (b) How many spare bottles of milk were there ?

7. In one day a clothing shop sold: 3 suits costing £87 each, 5 coats costing £59 each, and 10 pairs of trousers costing £24 each. How much money was taken for the total sales that day ?

8. A steel bar is 832 mm long.
   (a) How many pieces, each 16 mm long can be cut from the bar ?
   (b) How many steel bars of the same length would be needed to produce 250 16 mm pieces ?

THE DECIMAL SYSTEM

The first thing you read in this book was that our number system is called the decimal system, and it is based on the number ten. The present topic, decimal fractions, follows automatically from our ordinary way of writing numbers.

When we write the number: 333, we understand that it means: 300 + 30 + 3.
Reading from right to left, each digit is ten times the value of the previous one.
Reading from left to right, each digit is *one tenth* the value of the previous one.

In fact we can continue with the system to make fractions - parts of whole numbers.

Look at this number: 3 3 3 . 3 3

Especially notice the dot or full stop. This is a decimal point. It separates whole numbers from fractions.
All the numbers to the right of the decimal point are decimal fractions.

We read this number as: three hundred and thirty-three *point* three three.
Just as we count in tens in the decimal system, so decimal fractions are in parts of ten.
Look at how it works in columns:

100s	10s	units		10ths	100ths
3	3	3	.	3	3

The decimal point makes the system very easy, for we can always see immediately the value of the figures on either side of it.
We can write out a whole series of number values for whole numbers and fractions:

WHOLE NUMBERS						.	FRACTIONS			
100Th	10Th	Th	H	T	U	.	$^1/_{10}$	$^1/_{100}$	$^1/_{1\,000}$	$^1/_{10\,000}$

Example 1

How to write out decimal fractions:

(a)	fourteen and eight tenths:	1 4 . 8
(b)	three hundred and eight and eight hundredths:	3 0 8 . 0 8
(c)	One thousand and forty, five tenths and six thousandths:	1 0 4 0 . 5 0 6

Notice that it is important to put a zero in any empty column inside a decimal fraction. In example (b) there are no tenths, so we must enter a zero in the tenths column. In example (c) there has to be a zero in the hundredths column.

Exercise 9

Write out the following as decimal fractions:

1.   19 and 8 tenths   2.   25 and 6 hundredths   3. $289^7/_{10}$

4. $99^{13}/_{100}$ 5.   two thousand and eighteen, and nine tenths

6.   289 and seven thousandths   7.   no whole numbers, and three tenths

8. $^{55}/_{1\ 000}$ 9.   nine hundredths

10.   fourteen thousand, and four thousandths.

You will have noticed in this exercise how we can write decimal fractions with the digit of the fractional number above the tenths or hundredths or thousandths.

Example 2

(a) $^5/_{10}$ (five tenths)

(b) $9\ ^1/_{100}$ (nine, and one hundredth)

(c) $300\ ^9/_{1\ 000}$ (three hundred, and nine thousandths)

(d) $10^{24}/_{100}$ (ten, and two tenths and four hundredths)*

(e) $30^1/_{1\ 000}$ (three tenths, no hundredths, one thousandth)*

Fractions written this way are sometimes called *vulgar fractions*; and when they have a whole number with them they are called *mixed numbers*.

*Notice how we could describe these fractions in a different way:

(d)   Instead of two tenths and four hundredths, we could write:

twenty four hundredths.

(e)   Instead of three tenths, no hundredths, one thousandth, we could write:

three hundred and one thousandths.

These fractional numbers are very hard to say in words, and the decimal system is much simpler.
We can read example (d) as: ten point two four;
We can read example (e) as: nought point three nought one (or even just: point three nought one).

Exercise 9A

Change the following decimal fractions into vulgar fractions or mixed numbers:

1.	4.9	2.	77.93	3.	127.89	4.	66.7	5.	91.08
6.	277.76	7.	5 000.7	8.	20.027	9.	0.9	10.	0.003

THE FOUR RULES OF DECIMALS

ADDITION AND SUBTRACTION OF DECIMALS

This is done in exactly the same way as the addition and subtraction of whole numbers.

Care must be taken that the decimal points are all written directly over and each other. This ensures that the columns are properly set out, and digits of the same place value are all the correct columns. It is equally important to put the decimal point in the answer directly under the decimal points in the question.

Example 1

$11.68 + 5.076 + 21.5$

```
      1 1 . 6 8
  +     5 . 0 7 6
      2 1 . 5
  _____
      3 8 . 2 5 6
  _____
          1     1
```

Example 2

Subtract 15.85 from 28.2

```
    2   ⁷8 . ¹2   ¹0
  -  1  5 . 8   5
  _____
     1  2 . 3   5
  _____
```

In order to carry out this subtraction we need to insert a zero at the end of the figure 28.2. Zeros following at the end (on the right) of a decimal fraction do not change the value of the fraction. They can be inserted or left out as is convenient. Zeros in the middle or at the beginning of decimal fractions are very important, however. If we left out the zero in 5.076, we would change its value.

When a decimal fraction has no whole number part, in order to avoid mistakes a zero is usually written before the decimal point (on the left). Therefore: .625 would usually be written 0.625.

With a whole number without a decimal fraction, it is convenient to follow it with the decimal point, and a series of zeros. These do not change its value since they follow the decimal point. They mean that there are no tenths, no hundredths, and so on. They are only written to help in setting out the calculation. So if we were adding: .035 and 72, we would write the two numbers as: 0.035 and 72.000.

Example 5

Add together: 0.03, .3 and 33.

```
     0 . 0 3
 +   0 . 3 0
   3 3 . 0 0
  _____
   3 3 . 3 3
  _____
```

Example 5 A

Find the difference between 8.95 and 55.

```
   5 5 . 0 0
 +   8 . 9 5
  _____
   4 6 . 0 5
  _____
```

Look through these two examples, and see how many zeros have been added for convenience - that is zeros which do not change the value of the figures.

Exercise 10

Set out the following addition sums correctly and work out the answers:

1.   273.5 + 123.9
2.   91.83 + 81.87
3.   2.73 + 27.3 + 0.273
4.   503 + 71.25 + 19.2
5.   395 + 3.95 + 0.0395
6.   12.5 + 265 + 0.875
7.   1.9 + 18.3 + 135.5
8.   155 + 21 + 8005.315
9.   71.7 + 0.7 + 0.77 + 17
10.   99 + 9.9 + 0.99 + 0.099

Exercise 10 A

Set out the following subtractions correctly and work out the answers:

1.   20.2 - 16.5
2.   109.5 - 88.7
3.   17 - 8.45
4.   21.3 - 3.58
5.   12.5 - 7.69
6.   38.0 - 19.05
7.   7.071 - 6.325
8.   0.9054 - 0.1763
9.   1006 - 238.51
10.   3.0269 - 0.987

MULTIPLICATION OF DECIMALS

The simplest method for the multiplication of decimals is as follows:

(a)   Set the sum out as for an ordinary (short or long) multiplication.

(b)   Go ahead and do the sum as if it were an ordinary multiplication.

(c)   Completely ignore the decimal points until you have the full result.

(d)   Then count up the total number of digits to the right of the decimal point in each of the two numbers you multiplied together.

(e)   In the product (the answer to a multiplication sum), count the same number of digits from the right, and then insert the decimal point to the left of the last number you counted.

Look at how this works in the following examples:

Example 4

2.63 x 7   (a) Without decimal point

```
      2 6 3
   x      7
   _____
   1 8 4 1
   _____
     1  4  2
```

(b) Insert decimal point (after two digits)

```
      2 . 6 3
   x        7
   _____
   1 8 . 4 1
   _____
```

There are two places of decimals in 2.63, and none in 7. So we count two places from the right, and insert the decimal point, to give the answer 18.41.

Example 4a

5.032 x 24   (a) Without decimal point

```
       5 0 3 2
   x      2 4
   _____
     2 0 1 2 8
       2    1
   1 0 0 6 4 0
     1
   _____
   1 2 0 7 6 8
   _____
```

(b) Insert decimal point (after three digits)

```
       5 . 0 3 2
   x        2 4
   _____
     2 0   1 2 8
   1 0 0   6 4 0
   _____
   1 2 0 . 7 6 8
   _____
```

19

Example 4 b

In this example, both the numbers we are multiplying have decimal fractions, but this does not affect the method we use.

4.12 x 2.06

(a) Without decimal point   (b) Insert decimal point

```
        4 1 2                              4 . 1   2
    x   2 0 6                          x   2 . 0   6
    _____                          _____
        2 4 7 2                          2   4 7   2
          ² ¹
        8 2 4 0 0                        8   2 4 0 0
    _____                          _____
    1 2 0 7 6 8                          8 . 4 8   7   2
    _____                          _____
```

Notice that there are two places of decimals in the first number we are multiplying, and also two places of decimals in the second number. So in the answer we must have 2 + 2 = 4 places of decimals.

Checking the Decimal Point Position in Multiplication

There is a way to check that your answer is roughly right, and in particular to make sure that you have not placed the decimal point incorrectly. The method is to multiply together the whole numbers in the question only. This will give you an approximate answer.

So in example (a) 2.63 x 7, we can multiply 7 x 2 (ignoring the .63). The answer is 14.
Our final answer was 18, so we know that we are quite likely to be right.

In example (b) the two whole numbers (ignoring the decimal fraction) are 5 and 24. 5 x 24 = 120
Our final answer was 120.768, which is just over 120, and therefore probably correct.

In example (c) we have 4 x 2 = 8 as the multiplication of the whole numbers only, and since our answer was 8.4872, we are once again likely to be correct.

Exercise 11

Set out these multiplication sums correctly, and work out the answers.

1.	52. 8 x 5	2.	301.6 x 9	3.	20.25 x 6	4.	2.095 x 8
5.	51.92 x 16	6.	20.3 x 21	7.	92.6 x 32	8.	7.6 x 4.3
9.	32.13 x 2.09	10.	29.52 x 6.34				

20

DIVISION OF DECIMALS   (a)   **Dividing by a whole number**

(1)   Set out the division sum exactly as you would in an ordinary division.

(2)   In the answer space insert the decimal point exactly above the decimal point in the number to be divided (the dividend)

(3)   Divide in the usual way, without touching the decimal point.

Example 7

9.72 ÷ 9

```
          1  .  0   8
         ────────────
     9 ) 9  .  7  ⁷2
```

Example 7a

8.48 ÷ 16

```
          0  .  5   3
         ────────────
  1  6 ) 8  .  4   8
          8  .  0
         ────────
             .  4   8
             .  4   8
            ─────────
                0
```

Notice that when you are doing the working out of the division sum you ignore the decimal point, and carry on just as if you were dealing with whole numbers. So long as you know your tables, and know the method for short division (as in example (a)) and long division (as in example (b)), you should not have any difficulties with division of decimals.

However, the decimal point in the answer is vital, and you must not forget it, or move it.

Exercise 12

Set out the following division sums correctly and work out the answers:

1.	13.6 ÷ 4	2.	27.6 ÷ 6	3.	4.98 ÷ 6	4.	0.728 ÷ 4
5.	1.128 ÷ 12	6.	19.84 ÷ 16	7.	17.5 ÷ 14	8.	63.52 ÷ 21
9.	1266.3 ÷ 42	10.	0.4 ÷ 80				

DIVISION OF DECIMALS   (b)   Dividing by a decimal fraction

The method for dividing by a decimal is to change the decimal into a whole number.

Every decimal can be made into a whole number by multiplying it by ten (if it is tenths), or by a hundred (if it is hundredths), and so on.

To multiply a decimal by ten, move the digits one place to the left, across the decimal point.
To multiply a decimal by a hundred, move the digits two places to the left, across the point, and so on.

There is one other important step to remember:
What you do to the divisor (the number you are dividing by), you must also do to the dividend (the number you are dividing into). So if you multiply the divisor by ten, you must also multiply the dividend by ten. You do it in exactly the same way by moving the digits to the left across the decimal point.

Example 6

3.68 ÷ 0.8

The first thing to do is make 0.8 into a whole number.
Multiply it by ten, by moving the digits one place to the left across the decimal point. We now have 8.

Do the same thing to the dividend. So 3.68 now becomes 36.8

We can now employ the usual procedure to divide 36.8 by 8.

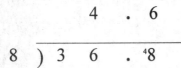

$$
\begin{array}{r}
4 \ . \ 6 \\
\hline
8 \ ) \ 3 \ 6 \ . \ ^48
\end{array}
$$

Example 6 a

0.496 ÷ 0.16

In this example we must multiply by 100, to change 0.16 into 16.

We must also remember to multiply 0.496 by 100 as well, so that it becomes 49.6 for the calculation.
We also have to use the long division method.

$$
\begin{array}{r}
0 \ 3 \ . \ 1 \\
\hline
1 \ 6 \ ) \ 4 \ 9 \ . \ 6 \\
4 \ 8 \ . \quad \\
\hline
1 \ . \ 6 \\
1 \ . \ 6 \\
\hline
0 \quad 0
\end{array}
$$

Example 6 b

Sometimes division sums are presented in this way:

$$\frac{2.468}{0.04}$$

With these sums all you have to remember is that the top line must be divided by the bottom line. (So the top line is the dividend, and the bottom line is the divisor.)

Carry out the usual procedures to make the divisor (the bottom line number) into a whole number. Here you have to move the digits two places to the left across the decimal point. This multiplies 0.04 by 100, and makes it: 4.
Do not forget to do the same to the top line. The digits move two places to the left across the decimal point again, multiplying them by 100, and the resulting figure is now: 246.8

Set the calculation out in the usual way:

```
              6   1  .  7
         _____
    4  ) 2   4   6  .  ²8
```

Sometimes the procedure of multiplying by ten or a hundred is described as moving the decimal point. In fact, however, the decimal point remains where it is, and the digits of the number move across it, changing their columns.

Exercise 12 A

Set out the following division sums correctly and work out the answers:

1.	$0.56 \div 0.8$	2.	$181.5 \div 0.5$	3.	$34.16 \div 0.8$
4.	$1.308 \div 1.2$	5.	$4.2 \div 0.35$	6.	$96.3 \div 0.9$

7. $\dfrac{2.4}{0.5}$ 8. $\dfrac{90}{1.2}$ 9. $\dfrac{0.126}{0.6}$ 10. $\dfrac{3.108}{1.5}$

Exercise 13 General Revision of Decimals (including problems)

1. Find the sum of 0.056, 3.42, and 10.01.
2. What is the difference between 3.9 and 9.3 ?
3. Find the product of 12.09 and 142.7
4. Share 29.82 by 14.
5. What is twelve and five tenths of 201 ?
6. How many times will 0.063 go into 97.839 ?
7. If the result of multiplying 2.397 by another number is 4.3146, what is the other number ?
8. There are 24 children in a class. 0.5 of this number are girls. How many boys are there ?
9. Add 0.75 to five hundredths, divide your result by two and then multiply it by 100.
10. If 0.25 of a number is 1.2, what is 0.75 of the number ?

FACTORS - AN INTRODUCTION TO FRACTIONS

FACTORS

A number is a factor of another number if it divides into that number exactly, with no remainder.

So, 8 is a factor of 48, because it divides exactly six times into 48. 48 is also exactly divisible (without a remainder) by: 1, 2, 3, 4, 6, 12, 16, 24, and 48 itself. All these numbers are factors of 48.

All numbers have themselves and one as factors. All even numbers also have 2 as a factor (because all even numbers are divisible by 2).

PRIME NUMBERS

As we have mentioned every number must have itself and one as a factor. There are some numbers which have no other factors at all. These are called prime numbers.

Although one is a factor of all the other numbers, it is not itself regarded as a prime number. The only even prime number is 2. All the other even numbers are divisible by 2, and therefore cannot be prime numbers.

PRIME FACTORS

A factor of a number may itself be a prime number. (As we have seen 2 is a factor of all the even numbers, and yet is itself a prime number.) When we have a factor which is also a prime number, it is known as a prime factor. For example, in the equation: 2 x 24 = 48, we know that 2 is a prime factor. 24 is a factor, but not a prime factor, as it has several factors of its own: 2, 3, 4, 6, 8, and 12. In the same way 21 has only two factors - seven and three, and both of these are in fact prime numbers, so they are both prime factors of 21.

HIGHEST COMMON FACTOR

The highest common factor is often shortened to H.C.F. The H.C.F. is the highest number which will divide exactly into two or more other numbers. It is the highest number which is a factor of those numbers. You can usually work out the H.C.F. of two or three simple numbers so long as you know your tables. The easiest way to do this is by trial and error. Try dividing numbers into each of those you are working with, to see which are factors.

For example, the H.C.F. of 36 and 54 is nine. This means that nine is the highest number which will divide into 36 and also into 54. There is no higher number which divides exactly into both. There are other common factors of both. Two and three and six all divide into both numbers exactly. But nine is the highest number which divides into both - the highest common factor.

LOWEST COMMON MULTIPLE

The lowest common multiple is often shortened to L.C.M. The multiples of a number are the things you learn in the times tables - except that they go on past ten times.

So the multiples of five are: 5, 10, 15, 20, 25, **30**, 35, 40, 45, 50, 55, **60**, and so on.
The multiples of six are: 6, 12, 18, 24, **30**, 36, 42, 48, 54, **60**, 66, 72, and so on.

You will have noticed that 30 and 60 appear in both lists. They are both multiples of both five and also of six. So they are both *common* multiples of five and six. The lowest common multiple of two or more numbers is the lowest number which is a multiple of the numbers concerned.

The L.C.M. of many numbers can be found simply by looking at them and by knowing your tables. The lowest common multiple of 5 and 6 happens to be the result of 5 x 6. If you need to work out a more complicated L.C.M. - especially one where you have three or more numbers involved, then the best method to use is to write out the multiplication tables for the numbers, and compare the figures.

Exercise 14

1.   List the factors of each of the following numbers, in ascending order (smallest first):
      (a)   32   (b)   45   (c)   26   (d)   60   (e)   72

2.   Write down all the prime numbers below 100.
      (Should you include 1 as a prime number ? Check back to the previous page if you are not sure.)

3.   Write down all of the prime factors for each of the following numbers:
      (a)   32   (b)   45   (c)   26   (d)   60   (e)   72

4.   Find the highest common factor (H.C.F.) of each of the following pairs of numbers:
      (a)   36 and 84   (b)   66 and 121   (c)   30 and 75   (d)   36 and 144

5.   Find the lowest common multiple (L.C.M.) of each of the following sets of numbers:
      (a)   6 and 9   (b)   2, 3 and 5   (c)   6 and 15   (d)   3, 5 and 10
      (e)   2, 3, 4 and 9

FRACTIONS

A fraction is a part of a whole number. You must imagine the whole number divided into a number of equal parts. The fraction then comprises a number of these parts.

This is a typical fraction: $^2/_3$

The top line is known as the numerator.
The bottom line is known as the denominator.

So in this case the numerator is two and the denominator is three.

The denominator tells us into how many equal parts the number has been divided.

The numerator tells us how many of those equal parts we are dealing with in the particular case.

Here is a diagram of how the fraction $^2/_3$ looks. The whole one has been divided into three equal parts. Two of these are shaded - that is two parts out of the three, or $^2/_3$. There is one part out of the three ($^1/_3$) left unshaded.

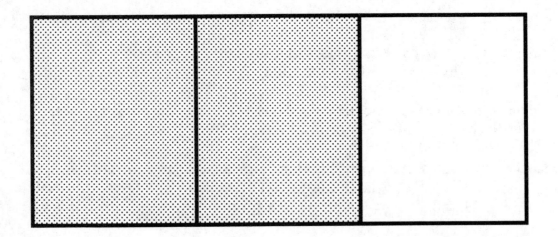

Exercise 15

Here are some more fractions. Draw diagrams to show the whole, the number of parts it has been divided into, and the number of parts which have been stated. You can show this last item by shading the correct number of parts, as in the diagram above.
Use 1 cm to represent each equal part in your drawings.

(1) $^5/_6$ (2) $^3/_4$ (3) $^7/_{10}$ (4) $^1/_5$ (5) $^2/_7$

(6) $^9/_{12}$ (7) $^5/_8$ (8) $^1/_6$ (9) $^2/_9$ (10) $^5/_{11}$

IMPROPER FRACTIONS AND MIXED NUMBERS

An improper fraction is a fraction in which the numerator (top line) is larger than the denominator (bottom line). What this means is that the fraction concerned is more than one. Or we could say that it is a whole number, or several whole numbers, plus some fractions.

These are improper fractions: $4/3$ $9/7$ $24/12$

A mixed number is a whole number with a fraction attached to it, like $2^2/3$ or $4^7/8$.

Changing Improper Fractions to Mixed Numbers

Here are some improper fractions. (The numerator is larger than the denominator.)

(a) $5/4$ (b) $6/5$ (c) $11/3$

This is how you can turn them into mixed numbers, by using a diagram method:

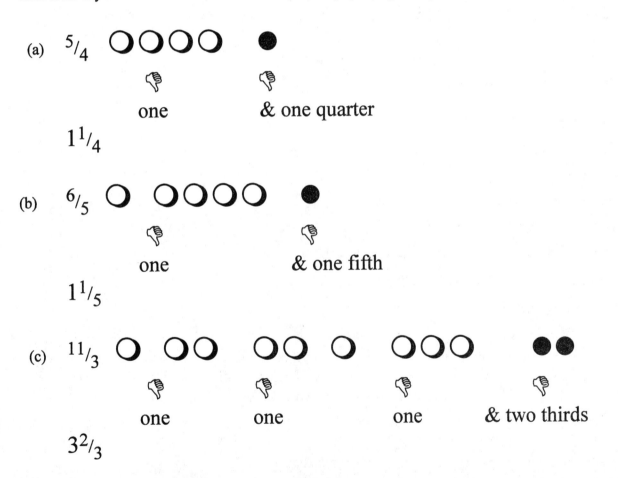

(a) $5/4$ one   & one quarter

$1^1/4$

(b) $6/5$ one   & one fifth

$1^1/5$

(c) $11/3$ one   one   one   & two thirds

$3^2/3$

There is also a short and simple way of working out these changes:

(1)   Divide the top line (numerator) of the improper fraction by the bottom line (denominator).

(2)   The result of the division is the whole number part of the mixed number.

(3)   The remainder is the fraction part of the mixed number, with the same denominator as before.

27

Exercise 16

Change the following improper fractions to mixed numbers. Use the diagram method, and then check your answer by the short method given at the bottom of the previous page.

(1) $^{7}/_{3}$ (2) $^{11}/_{4}$ (3) $^{12}/_{7}$ (4) $^{13}/_{5}$

(5) $^{21}/_{10}$ (6) $^{16}/_{7}$ (7) $^{19}/_{8}$ (8) $^{27}/_{8}$

(9) $^{43}/_{6}$ (10) $^{41}/_{6}$ (11) $^{31}/_{7}$ (12) $^{52}/_{9}$

Changing Mixed Numbers to Improper Fractions

The first step is to express the whole number part as if it were a fraction. Look at the denominator.
Each one whole number will have the same numerator as the denominator (like: $^{3}/_{3}$ or $^{4}/_{4}$ or $^{6}/_{6}$).

So if we have $1^{1}/_{3}$ the whole number (one) can be written as $^{3}/_{3}$. We already have another $^{1}/_{3}$
- so what we have altogether is $^{3}/_{3}$ + $^{1}/_{3}$ = $^{4}/_{3}$.

$1^{1}/_{3}$ written as an improper fraction is $^{4}/_{3}$.

Look at another mixed number: $2^{1}/_{2}$.
This time we have two ones (two whole numbers), both of which we want to write as fractions.
The denominator we are looking at is 2.
The first one (whole number) can be written as: $^{2}/_{2}$.
The second one (whole number) can also be written as: $^{2}/_{2}$.
We already have the $^{1}/_{2}$ from the original mixed number.
Add them all together and we get this equation: $^{2}/_{2}$ + $^{2}/_{2}$ + $^{1}/_{2}$ = $^{5}/_{2}$.
$2^{1}/_{2}$ written as an improper fraction is $^{5}/_{2}$.

So long as you remember that each whole number can be written in the form of a fraction with the same numerator and the same denominator, you should not find this method difficult. Write one of these strange fractions for each whole number in the mixed number - and do not forget to add on the original fraction from the mixed number.

There is also a short and simple way of working out these changes:

(1)   Multiply the whole number by the denominator (bottom line) of the fraction.

(2)   Add the numerator (top line) of the fraction to your result.

(3)   Write the total over the original denominator.

Exercise 16 A

Change the following improper fractions to mixed numbers. Use the diagram method, and then check your answer by the short method given at the bottom of the previous page.

(1) $1\,^5/_8$ (2) $2\,^5/_9$ (3) $1\,^7/_{10}$ (4) $3\,^3/_4$

(5) $5\,^1/_5$ (6) $3\,^7/_{11}$ (7) $2\,^9/_{12}$ (8) $6\,^6/_7$

(9) $3\,^7/_{13}$ (10) $9\,^1/_2$ (11) $8\,^1/_7$ (12) $7\,^5/_8$

EQUIVALENT FRACTIONS

There are many ways of writing the same fraction:

$$^1/_3 \;=\; ^3/_9 \;=\; ^2/_6 \;=\; ^4/_{12}$$

$$^3/_4 \;=\; ^6/_8 \;=\; ^{18}/_{24} \;=\; ^{15}/_{20}$$

You will sometimes be asked to find an equivalent fraction. These examples show how it is done.

(a) $^1/_2 \;=\; ^7/_\square$

One over two (a half) equals seven over.......what ?

$$\overset{\text{☞ } 7\,x}{^1/_2 \;=\; ^7/_\square} \quad \Rightarrow \quad ^7/_{14}$$
$$7\,x \text{ ☞}$$

The seven on the top line is seven times bigger than the one.
What happens on the top line must also happen on the bottom line.
So what is seven times bigger than the two on the bottom line ? Answer: 7 x 2 = 14

(b) $^2/_\square \;=\; ^{16}/_{24}$

Two over.....something..... equals sixteen over 24.

$$\overset{8\,x \text{ ☞}}{^2/_\square \;=\; ^{16}/_{24}} \Rightarrow \;^2/_3$$
$$\text{☞ } 8\,x$$

The sixteen on the top line is eight times bigger than the two.
What happens on the top line must also happen on the bottom line.
So what number is the 24 on the bottom line eight times bigger than ? 24 ÷ 8 = 3

(c) $4/5 = \square/20$

Can you do this one ?

The twenty on the bottom line is four times bigger than the five on the bottom line.
What happens on the bottom line must also happen on the top line.
So what is four times bigger than the 4 on the top line ?

Exercise 17

Work out these equivalent fractions by the same method.

(1) $5/9 = 35/\square$ (2) $1/3 = \square/12$ (3) $4/7 = 16/\square$

(4) $1/8 = 9/\square$ (5) $4/9 = 36/\square$ (6) $2/5 = \square/30$

(7) $2/6 = 8/\square$ (8) $\square/10 = 2/5$

CANCELLING

As we have already seen, there are many ways of writing the same fraction. When you are working with fractions, you often want to use the simplest equivalent form possible. To do this you can *cancel* fractions, or *simplify* them to their lowest terms.

The way to do this is to divide both the numerator and denominator by the same number.

You need to find the smallest number that goes into each exactly - the Highest Common Factor (H.C.F.) Check back to *Topic Four* on page 24 and read the section on H.C.F.'s again.

Look at these examples of cancelling or simplifying fractions:

(a)   ☞   factors of 9 are......... 1 **3** 9

$9/12$

       ☞ factors of 12 are........ 1 2 **3** 4 6 12

The highest common factor (in fact the only common factor) of 9 and 12 is 3.
So you can divide both parts of the fraction by 3:

     $9 \div 3 = 3$ (the numerator)
     $12 \div 3 = 4$ (the denominator)

$9/12 = 3/4$

(b) ☞ factors of 12 are......... 1 **2 3 4 6 12**

$^{12}/_{24}$

☞ factors of 24 are........ 1 **2 3 4 6** 8 **12** 24

There are plenty of common factors in this example, but we are looking for the highest: 12.
So you can divide both parts of the fraction by 12:

$12 \div 12 = 1$ (the numerator)
$24 \div 12 = 2$ (the denominator)

$^{12}/_{24} = ^{1}/_{2}$

It is often possible to cancel fractions you are using in calculations simply by looking at them.
The cancellation can be carried out by striking out the original numbers and replacing them with
smaller numbers like this:

$^{1}\cancel{12}/\cancel{24}_{2}$

If you find you have difficulty working out the H.C.F. of the denominator and numerator of the fraction,
you may be able to notice a simple cancellation that you can carry out. For example if both numbers are
even, you can simply divide both by two. Also, after a first cancellation you may notice another.
By cancelling a fraction several times using low numbers as the factors you divide by, you can still get
to the same result.

In example (b), you might therefore divide first by 2, which would give us:

$^{12}/_{24} = ^{6}/_{12}$

You would probably then notice that six and twelve are both divisible by 6, to give you the same
final result: $^{1}/_{2}$

We could even show it like this:

$^{1\,6}\cancel{12}/\cancel{24}\ _{\cancel{12}\ 2}$

Exercise 18

Simplify these fractions to their lowest terms by cancelling:

(1) $^{5}/_{15}$ (2) $^{12}/_{18}$ (3) $^{10}/_{30}$ (4) $^{16}/_{20}$ (5) $^{15}/_{21}$

(6) $^{20}/_{25}$ (7) $^{18}/_{21}$ (8) $^{30}/_{35}$ (9) $^{42}/_{48}$ (10) $^{24}/_{96}$

CHANGING VULGAR FRACTIONS INTO DECIMALS

What you are doing here is changing one sort of fraction into its equivalent as another sort of fraction (a decimal fraction).

The method is simple. You divide the top line of the fraction (the numerator) by the bottom line of the fraction (the denominator).

When you write out the division sum, you will need to show the numerator with a decimal point followed by some zeros. This is the normal way of setting out a decimal division sum. Check back to page 21 where the method is fully explained. The following examples show you how it works:

Example (a)

Change $^1/_2$ into a decimal fraction.

$$\begin{array}{r} 0 \; . \; 5 \\ \hline 2 \,) \; 1 \; . \; {}^1 0 \end{array}$$

In this division the numerator of the fraction (1) becomes the dividend, shown as: 1.0
The denominator of the fraction becomes the divisor (2).

Answer: $^1/_2$ = 0.5

Example (b)

Change $^3/_8$ into a decimal fraction.

$$\begin{array}{r} 0 \; . \; 3 \; 7 \; 5 \\ \hline 8 \,) \, 3 \; . \; {}^3 0 \; {}^6 0 \; {}^4 0 \end{array}$$

Answer: $^3/_8$ = 0.375

Example (c)

Sometimes the answers do not work out exactly. It is then usual to take the answer as far as three decimal places (to the thousandths column), as shown in this example.

Change $^9/_{11}$ into a decimal fraction.

$$\begin{array}{r} 0 \; . \; 8 \; 1 \; 8 \\ \hline 1 \, 1 \,) \, 9 \; . \; {}^9 0 \; {}^2 0 \; {}^9 0 \end{array}$$

Answer: $^9/_{11}$ = 0.818

If we kept on dividing, the sum would go on forever: 0.818181818181........ !

Exercise 19

Change the following into decimal fractions:

(1) $3/5$ (2) $7/8$ (3) $3/4$ (4) $19/20$ (5) $9/10$

(6) $5/8$ (7) $16/25$ (8) $17/23$ (9) $19/24$ (10) $2/3$

Notice that for some of the questions you will have to use the method for long division of decimals. There is an example on Page 22 if you want to check it.

CHANGING DECIMALS INTO VULGAR FRACTIONS

What you are doing here is once again changing one sort of fraction(a decimal fraction) into its equivalent as another sort of fraction. It is the opposite of the conversion you have just learnt.

The method this time is much simpler, however.

Firstly write the decimal as a fraction with tenths, hundredths, thousandths etc. as the denominator. Then cancel the fraction, if that is possible.

For example:

Change 0.75 to a vulgar fraction.

First we write it as a fraction: 75 hundredths, or: $75/100$.

Now we try to find the H.C.F. of 75 and 100. In fact the H.C.F. is 25, but you may not manage to work that out, and may have to cancel first by 5, and then , giving a result something like this:

$$^{3}\ ^{15}\ ^{\cancel{75}}/_{\cancel{100}\ _{20}\ _{4}}$$

So: $0.75 = 75/100 = 3/4$.

If you cannot cancel, then leave the fraction in its original form; it is still a vulgar fraction.

Exercise 20

Change the following into vulgar fractions, and reduce them to their lowest terms by cancelling where this is possible:

(1) 0.25   (2) 0.4   (3) 0.9   (4) 0.625
(5) 0.5   (6) 0.45   (7) 0.103   (8) 1.8

33

THE FOUR RULES OF FRACTIONS

ADDITION OF FRACTIONS

When you are adding fractions which have the same denominator (bottom line), the method is very simple. You add the numerators (top lines), and put the result over the denominator. Do NOT add the denominators.

Example (a)

Add $^2/_5$ and $^1/_5$.   Answer: $^3/_5$ (not $^3/_{10}$).

When you are adding fractions with different denominators, the process becomes much more complicated, and you have to begin by finding the L.C.M. (lowest common multiple) of the denominators. This is sometimes known as the *common denominator*.

Check back to page 25 if you are not sure what the L.C.M. is and how to find it.

Once you have found the L.C.M. you convert each of the fractions to be added to the equivalent fraction using the L.C.M. as the new denominator.

Check back to pages 29 and 30 for how to do equivalent fractions.

You can then proceed to add the two fractions as in *example (a)* above.

Example (b)

Add $^2/_5$ and $^1/_3$.

Multiples of 5:   5   10   **15**
Multiples of 3:   3   6   9   12   **15**

We soon see that the L.C.M. of 3 and 5 is 15. (In fact 15 is the product of 3 and 5.)
So 15 becomes the new denominator

We now need work out the new numerators for each fraction:

$$^2/_5 = \Box/_{15} \Rightarrow \quad ^6/_{15} \qquad\qquad ^1/_3 = \Box/_{15} \Rightarrow \quad ^5/_{15}$$

(☞ 3 x ... 3 x ☞)   (☞ 5 x ... 5 x ☞)

Now we have the simple addition to perform: $^6/_{15} + ^5/_{15} = ^{11}/_{15}$

Example (c)

Add $^5/_6$ and $^4/_9$.

Multiples of 6:   6 12 **18**
Multiples of 9:   9 **18**

So the L.C.M. of 6 and 9 is 18.
This means that 18 becomes the new denominator

We now need work out the new numerators for each fraction as in the previous example:

☞ 3 x   ☞ 2 x

$^5/_6$ = $\square/_{18}$ $\Rightarrow$ $^{15}/_{18}$ $^4/_9$ = $\square/_{18}$ $\Rightarrow$ $^8/_{18}$

3 x ☞   2 x ☞

Now we have the simple addition to perform: $^{15}/_{18}$ + $^8/_{18}$ = $^{23}/_{18}$

In this example there is one further step.

The numerator of this fraction is larger than the denominator. So the answer is at the moment in the form of an improper fraction.

It should be converted into a mixed number by dividing the numerator by the denominator:
23 ÷ 18 = 1 r. 5.

The one is the whole number, with a remainder of five eighteenths.

So the answer correctly stated as a mixed number is: $1^5/_{18}$

Exercise 21

Carry out the following additions of fractions:

(1) $^6/_7$ + $^1/_2$ (2) $^4/_5$ + $^2/_3$ (3) $^7/_{10}$ + $^1/_2$

(4) $^4/_5$ + $^1/_2$ (5) $^3/_4$ + $^2/_5$ (6) $^7/_9$ + $^5/_6$

(7) $^3/_4$ + $^7/_8$ (8) $^{11}/_{12}$ + $^4/_5$ (9) $^4/_7$ + $^2/_5$

(10) $^8/_9$ + $^1/_{12}$ (11) $^8/_{11}$ + $^1/_4$ (12) $^7/_{10}$ + $^2/_3$

SUBTRACTION OF FRACTIONS

The procedures for the subtraction of fractions are the same as those for addition. The only difference is that you must subtract instead of adding.

When you are subtracting fractions which have the same denominator (bottom line), you subtract the numerators (top lines), and put the result over the denominator. Do NOT try to subtract the denominators (which would always give you a denominator of zero).

Example (a)

Subtract $^2/_7$ from $^6/_7$.   Answer: $^4/_7$.

When you are subtracting fractions with different denominators, the process is more complicated, and once again you have to begin by finding the L.C.M. (lowest common multiple) of the denominators.

Once you have found the L.C.M. you convert each of the fractions to be subtracted to the equivalent fraction using the L.C.M. as the new denominator.

You can then proceed to subtract the two fractions as in *example (a)* above.

Example (b)

Subtract $^1/_{12}$ from $^3/_4$.

Multiples of 4:   4 8 **12**
Multiples of 12: **12**

The L.C.M. of 12 and 4 is in fact 12 itself. So 12 becomes the new denominator for both fractions.

(Notice how important it is to find the L.C.M., so that you get the lowest common denominator. If you just multiplied 4 by 12, you would have much more complicated working out with a denominator of 48.)

So, since the denominator is 12, the fraction $^1/_{12}$ remains as it was before, and we only need to work out a new numerator for $^3/_4$:

$$ ^3/_4 = ^\square/_{12} \quad \Rightarrow \quad ^9/_{12} $$

3 x (above) · 3 x (below)

Now we have the subtraction itself to perform: $^9/_{12} - ^1/_{12} = ^8/_{12}$.

In this example there is one further step. The answer to any calculation involving fractions should be given in its lowest terms. This means that if it can be cancelled, it should be.

The fraction $^8/_{12}$ can be cancelled by 4 : $^{2}8/_{12}_{3}$ So the final answer is: $^2/_3$

Exercise 22

Carry out the following subtractions of fractions:

(1) $\frac{7}{10} - \frac{1}{5}$ (2) $\frac{4}{7} - \frac{1}{2}$ (3) $\frac{6}{11} - \frac{1}{3}$

(4) $\frac{4}{5} - \frac{1}{2}$ (5) $\frac{9}{10} - \frac{2}{3}$ (6) $\frac{7}{8} - \frac{1}{4}$

(7) $\frac{5}{6} - \frac{1}{5}$ (8) $\frac{6}{7} - \frac{1}{3}$ (9) $\frac{9}{11} - \frac{1}{4}$

(10) $\frac{11}{12} - \frac{2}{5}$ (11) $\frac{3}{8} - \frac{1}{12}$ (12) $\frac{5}{9} - \frac{1}{6}$

ADDITION AND SUBTRACTION OF MIXED NUMBERS

In addition and subtraction of mixed numbers, we always deal with the whole numbers first.

Perform the addition or subtraction with the whole numbers.

Then perform the addition or subtraction with the fractions.

Simplify the answer (if possible) by cancelling.

Addition

Example (d)

Add $2\frac{1}{2}$ and $3\frac{1}{4}$.

The addition of whole numbers gives us: $2 + 3 = 5$

In adding the fractions we have an obvious L.C.M. of 4, which is the common denominator.

So $\frac{1}{2}$ becomes $\frac{2}{4}$ and $\frac{1}{4}$ stays the same: $\frac{2}{4} + \frac{1}{4} = \frac{3}{4}$

Now we put the whole number result and the fraction result together: $5\frac{3}{4}$

Example (e)

Add $4\frac{5}{6}$ and $2\frac{3}{4}$.

The addition of whole numbers gives us: $4 + 2 = 6$

Then we go on to the addition of the fractions.

Multiples of 6:   6 **12**
Multiples of 4: 4 8 **12**
So the L.C.M., 12, becomes the new denominator for both fractions.

Work out the two new fractions in the normal way, and you will get the result:

$$^{10}/_{12} \ + \ ^{9}/_{12} \ = \ ^{19}/_{12}$$

As you can see, the result is an improper fraction, and you must convert this to a mixed number:

$$^{19}/_{12} \ = \ 1\,^{7}/_{12} \ .$$

There is now one extra step to perform. You must add this mixed number to the original result of the addition of whole number:

$$6 + 1\,^{7}/_{12} \ = \ 7\,^{7}/_{12}$$

Exercise 23

Carry out the following additions of mixed numbers:

(1) $2\,^{1}/_{3} \ + \ 3\,^{3}/_{4}$ (2) $3\,^{2}/_{3} \ + \ 5\,^{8}/_{9}$ (3) $8\,^{1}/_{5} \ + \ 2\,^{1}/_{6}$

(4) $7\,^{6}/_{11} \ + \ 9\,^{21}/_{22}$ (5) $1\,^{5}/_{9} \ + \ 3\,^{3}/_{4}$ (6) $8\,^{1}/_{5} \ + \ ^{6}/_{2}$

(7) $4\,^{3}/_{8} \ + \ 1\,^{2}/_{3}$ (8) $5\,^{6}/_{2} \ + \ 2\,^{1}/_{3}$

Subtraction

Example (f)

Subtract $1\,^{1}/_{5}$ from $3\,^{2}/_{3}$.

The subtraction of whole numbers gives us: 3 - 1 = 2

Now we work out the fractions.
        Multiples of 3: 3 6 9 12 **15**
        Multiples of 5: 5 10 **15**
So the L.C.M., 15, becomes the new denominator for both fractions.

Calculate the two new fractions in the normal way, and perform the subtraction:

$$^{10}/_{15} \ - \ ^{3}/_{15} \ = \ ^{7}/_{15}$$

Now we put the whole number result and the fraction result together: $2\,^{7}/_{15}$

Example (g)

Subtract $5\,^4/_5$ from $9\,^1/_{10}$.

The subtraction of whole numbers gives us: $9 - 5 = 4$

In subtracting the fractions we have an obvious L.C.M. of 10, which is the common denominator.

So $^1/_{10}$ stays the same and $^4/_5$ becomes $^8/_{10}$: $^1/_{10}$ - $^8/_{10}$ = ?

As you can see we have a problem here. We cannot subtract $^8/_{10}$ from $^1/_{10}$.

What we have to do is the same sort of thing as we do when we are trying to subtract a larger number from a smaller one in ordinary subtraction: we borrow.

We borrow one from the whole number result. So the 4 whole ones now become 3.
We convert the one we have borrowed into a fraction. In this case we need it as tenths: $1 = \,^{10}/_{10}$

Then we add the ten tenths we have borrowed onto the fraction we are subtracting from:

$^1/_{10}$ + $^{10}/_{10}$ = $^{11}/_{10}$.

Now we can go ahead and carry out the subtraction:

$^{11}/_{10}$ - $^8/_{10}$ = $^3/_{10}$.

Finally the result of the subtraction of fractions can be put together with the result of the subtraction of whole number. Remember that you have reduced the whole number result by one in order to borrow.

$9\,^1/_{10}$ - $5\,^4/_5$ = $3\,^3/_{10}$

When the whole number is the answer is one, and you borrow it for the subtraction of fractions, you are left with zero, and therefore your answer will be a fraction alone, not a mixed number.

Exercise 23 A

Carry out the following subtractions of mixed numbers

(1) $5\,^2/_3$ - $1\,^1/_6$ (2) $6\,^3/_7$ - $4\,^7/_{21}$ (3) $6\,^4/_5$ - $2\,^{21}/_{25}$

(4) $1\,^1/_8$ - $^{15}/_{16}$ (5) $5\,^1/_9$ - $3\,^1/_4$ (6) $4\,^1/_9$ - $3\,^8/_9$

(7) $11\,^1/_2$ - $10\,^7/_8$ (8) $26\,^1/_5$ - $2\,^{14}/_{15}$

MULTIPLICATION OF FRACTIONS

The method for the multiplication of fractions is very simple:

> Multiply the numerators (top lines) together
> Multiply the denominators (bottom lines) together.

You can then simplify the answer (if possible) by cancelling.

Example (h)

Multiply $^2/_5$ by $^3/_7$.

The multiplication of the top line: 2 x 3 = 6.
The multiplication of the bottom line: 5 x 7 = 35.

Result: $^2/_5$ x $^3/_7$ = $^6/_{35}$

In the above example the result cannot be cancelled.

In some multiplications of fractions, it is possible to cancel before starting the calculation, in order to make the process simpler.

Look carefully at the numerators and the denominators.

Find a number which will divide equally into any one denominator and any one numerator.
They do not have to be the denominator and numerator of the same fraction.
Cancel the fractions concerned by this number.

Example (i)

Multiply $^2/_3$ by $^3/_5$.

You can cancel the denominator of $^3/_5$ and the numerator of $^2/_3$ (both 3):

$$^2/_{3_1} \ \ x \ \ ^{1}3/_5$$

Now carry on with the multiplication:

The multiplication of the top line: 2 x 1 = 2.
The multiplication of the bottom line: 1 x 5 = 5.

Result: $^2/_5$

You may also find multiplication sums where you can cancel by more than one number, as in the example on the following page.

Example (j)

Multiply $^5/_6$ by $^9/_{10}$.

You can cancel the denominator of $^5/_6$ and the numerator of $^9/_{10}$ (both are divisible by 3).

You can cancel the denominator of $^9/_{10}$ and the numerator of $^5/_6$ (both are divisible by 5).

$$^1\!\!\!\not5/_{\not6_2} \quad \text{x} \quad ^3\!\!\!\not9/_{\not{10}_2}$$

Now carry on with the multiplication:

The multiplication of the top line: 1 x 3 = 3.
The multiplication of the bottom line: 2 x 2 = 4.

Result: $^3/_4$

Example (k)

Here are two multiplication of fraction sums with their answers.

Write them out again in full showing how the fractions can be cancelled to make the multiplication easy and lead to the correct answers:

(i) $^4/_7$ x $^{21}/_{32}$ (ii) $^3/_{11}$ x $^{22}/_{39}$

          Answer: $^3/_8$ Answer: $^2/_{13}$

In the following exercise try to cancel whenever possible, in the same way as the above example.

Always check your end result. If you have missed a possibility to cancel at some stage, it will still be there in the final fraction, which should always then be reduced to its simplest terms.

Exercise 24

Carry out the following multiplications of fractions, making sure that you cancel any fractions which can be cancelled before you perform the calculation:

(1) $^3/_8$ x $^4/_9$ (2) $^6/_7$ x $^7/_8$ (3) $^4/_5$ x $^5/_6$

(4) $^3/_4$ x $^4/_{15}$ (5) $^9/_{10}$ x $^2/_9$ (6) $^1/_7$ x $^{14}/_{15}$

(7) $^3/_{10}$ x $^5/_9$ (8) $^1/_3$ x $^6/_7$

DIVISION OF FRACTIONS

The method for the division of fractions follows from that for multiplication:

First turn the fraction on the *right* of the division sign upside down.
Change the division sign into a multiplication sign.
Carry out any cancelling which is possible.
Multiply the numerators (top lines) together.
Multiply the denominators (bottom lines) together.

Example (l)

Divide $^1/_5$ by $^1/_2$.

$^1/_5 \div ^1/_2$.

Turn the second number (the one on the right of the division sign) upside down and multiply:

$^1/_5 \times ^2/_1$.

In this example no numbers can be cancelled.

The multiplication of the top line: $1 \times 2 = 2$.
The multiplication of the bottom line: $5 \times 1 = 5$.

Result: $^1/_5 \div ^1/_2 = ^2/_5$

Example (m)

Divide $^1/_4$ by $^7/_8$.

$^1/_4 \div ^7/_8$.

Turn the second number (the one on the right of the division sign) upside down and multiply:

$^1/_4 \times ^8/_7$.

In this example we can cancel the 4 and the 8 by four:

$^1/_{4_1} \times \, ^{2}8/_7$

The multiplication of the top line: $1 \times 2 = 2$.
The multiplication of the bottom line: $1 \times 7 = 7$.

Result: $^1/_4 \div ^7/_8 = ^2/_7$

Example (n)

Divide $^4/_5$ by $^8/_{15}$.   Set out the division: $^4/_5 \div {}^8/_{15}$.

Turn the second fraction upside down and multiply:

$^4/_5$ x $^{15}/_8$.

In this example we can cancel twice (by 4, and by 5):

$^1\cancel{4}/_{\cancel{5}\,1}$ x $^{3}\cancel{15}/_{\cancel{8}\,2}$

Multiply the top line: 1 x 3 = 3; and the bottom line: 1 x 2 = 2.

$^1/_4 \div {}^7/_8 = {}^3/_2$

As you will notice, $^3/_2$ is an improper fraction. (The numerator is larger than the denominator.)
When you have an improper fraction in your answer you must always convert it to a mixed number.

Result: $^1/_4 \div {}^7/_8 = {}^3/_2 = 1^1/_2$

When the second fraction is smaller than the first in the division of decimals, the result will always be
a mixed number or a whole number. In the following example it is a whole number:

Example (o)

Divide $^1/_2$ by $^1/_4$ Set out the division: $^1/_2 \div {}^1/_4$

$^1/_2$ x $^4/_1$ Cancel where possible: $^1/_{\cancel{2}\,1}$ x $^2\cancel{4}/_1$

$^1/_{\cancel{2}\,1}$ x $^2\cancel{4}/_1$ = $^2/_1$ = 2

Exercise 25

Carry out the following divisions of fractions, making sure that you cancel any fractions which can be
cancelled before you perform the calculation:

(1) $^2/_3 \div {}^1/_2$ (2) $^3/_4 \div {}^{11}/_{12}$ (3) $^4/_5 \div {}^3/_{10}$

(4) $^3/_5 \div {}^3/_4$ (5) $^7/_{10} \div {}^3/_5$ (6) $^5/_9 \div {}^5/_6$

(7) $^1/_3 \div {}^4/_7$ (8) $^1/_2 \div {}^1/_2$

MULTIPLICATION AND DIVISION OF MIXED NUMBERS

Before you can do multiplication or division of mixed numbers you *must* change them to improper fractions. You then follow the normal rules for the multiplication and division of fractions.

Remember the short and simple way of converting mixed numbers into improper fractions (*page 28*):

Multiply the whole number by the denominator (bottom line) of the fraction.
Add the numerator (top line) of the fraction to your result.
Write the total over the original denominator.

Examples: $\quad 3\,^1/_3 \; = \; {}^{10}/_3 \qquad\qquad 5^1/_5 \; = \; {}^{26}/_5 \qquad\qquad 4^1/_4 \; = \; {}^{17}/_4$

Exercise 26   Conversion of Mixed Numbers to Improper Fractions - Revision

Convert the following mixed numbers into improper fractions:

(1) $\quad 1\,^1/_4$ (2) $\quad 7\,^1/_5$ (3) $\quad 2\,^2/_3$ (4) $\quad 6\,^3/_4$

(5) $\quad 4\,^5/_9$ (6) $\quad 7\,^7/_8$ (7) $\quad 8\,^9/_{10}$ (8) $\quad 9\,^4/_{11}$

Multiplication

The following examples show the procedure for multiplication of mixed numbers

Example (p)

Multiply $^4/_5$ by $3\,^1/_3$.   First set out the multiplication: $^4/_5 \;\; \text{x} \;\; 3\,^1/_3$

Then convert the mixed number into an improper fraction: $^4/_5 \;\; \text{x} \;\; ^7/_3$

Cancel wherever possible (in this case the 4 and the 2): $^{2}\!{}^4/_5 \;\; \text{x} \;\; ^7/_{2\,1}$

Carry out the multiplication: $^4/_5 \;\; \text{x} \;\; ^7/_3 \; = \; ^{14}/_5$

Convert the improper fraction back into a mixed number: $^{14}/_5 \; = \; 2\,^4/_5$.

Example (q)

Multiply $1\,^2/_5$ by $3\,^1/_3$.   First set out the multiplication: $1\,^2/_5 \;\; \text{x} \;\; 3\,^1/_3$

Convert the mixed numbers into improper fractions: $^7/_5 \;\; \text{x} \;\; ^{10}/_3$

Cancel wherever possible (in this case the 10 and the 5): $^7/_{5\,1} \;\; \text{x} \;\; ^{2}\!{}^{10}/_3$

Carry out the multiplication: $^7/_{5\,1} \;\; \text{x} \;\; ^{2}\!{}^{10}/_3 \; = \; ^{14}/_3 \; = \; 4\,^2/_3$.

Exercise 26 A

Carry out the following multiplications of mixed numbers:

(1) $1\frac{1}{2}$ x $2\frac{1}{7}$ (2) $2\frac{1}{7}$ x $4\frac{2}{3}$ (3) $1\frac{4}{5}$ x $3\frac{3}{4}$

(4) $1\frac{3}{10}$ x $1\frac{7}{8}$ (5) $1\frac{1}{20}$ x $3\frac{1}{3}$ (6) $6\frac{5}{12}$ x $3\frac{3}{11}$

(7) $2\frac{2}{5}$ x $3\frac{1}{3}$ (8) $2\frac{1}{2}$ x $5\frac{1}{3}$

Division

Remember that in division of fractions, you turn the second fraction upside down, and then multiply.

The following examples show the procedure for division of mixed numbers

Example (r)

Divide $\frac{7}{8}$ by $3\frac{1}{2}$. First set out the division: $\frac{7}{8} \div 3\frac{1}{2}$

Then convert the mixed number into an improper fraction: $\frac{7}{8} \div \frac{7}{2}$

Turn the second fraction upside down and change the sign to multiply: $\frac{7}{8}$ x $\frac{2}{7}$

Cancel wherever possible: $\frac{{}^{1}7}{8_{4}}$ x $\frac{{}^{1}2}{7_{1}}$

Carry out the multiplication: $\frac{{}^{1}7}{8_{4}}$ x $\frac{{}^{1}2}{7_{1}}$ = $\frac{1}{4}$

Example (s)

Divide $4\frac{1}{8}$ by $\frac{3}{4}$. First set out the division: $4\frac{1}{8} \div \frac{3}{4}$

Convert the mixed number into an improper fraction: $\frac{33}{8} \div \frac{3}{4}$

Turn the second fraction upside down and change the sign to multiply: $\frac{33}{8}$ x $\frac{4}{3}$

Cancel wherever possible: $\frac{{}^{11}33}{8_{2}}$ x $\frac{{}^{1}4}{3_{1}}$

Carry out the multiplication: $\frac{{}^{11}33}{8_{2}}$ x $\frac{{}^{1}4}{3_{1}}$ = $\frac{11}{2}$

Convert the improper fraction back into a mixed number: $\frac{11}{2}$ = $5\frac{1}{2}$.

Example (t)

Divide $13^3/_4$ by $2^1/_2$.   First set out the division: $13^3/_4 \div 2^3/_4$

Convert the mixed number into an improper fraction: $^{55}/_4 \div {^5}/_2$

Turn the second fraction upside down and change the sign to multiply: $^{55}/_4 \times {^2}/_5$

Cancel wherever possible: $^5\cancel{55}/_4{_2} \times {^1}\cancel{2}/_{\cancel{5}}{_1}$

Carry out the multiplication: $^5\cancel{55}/_4{_2} \times {^1}\cancel{2}/_{\cancel{5}}{_1} = {^{11}}/_2$

Convert the improper fraction back into a mixed number: $^{11}/_2 = 5^1/_2$.

Exercise 26 B

Carry out the following divisions of mixed numbers:

(1) $\quad 5^1/_3 \div 2^1/_2$ (2) $\quad 10 \div {^3}/_5$ (3) $\quad 13^1/_2 \div 1^1/_2$

(4) $\quad 4^1/_4 \div 17$ (5) $\quad ^5/_{27} \div 1^1/_9$ (6) $\quad 4^1/_7 \div {^{29}}/_{35}$

(7) $\quad ^5/_6 \div 8^1/_3$ (8) $\quad 5^5/_6 \div 3^1/_8$

FINDING A FRACTION OF A NUMBER

Remember that in maths the word **OF** always means multiply (*page 10*).

So when you are told to find a fraction *of* a number, you know that you must multiply the fraction and the number to find the result.

Example (u)

Find $^1/_3$ of 9.

First set the problem out as a simple multiplication sum.

You can write any whole number as a fraction over 1, and it is always easier to do so in calculations involving fractions:

$^1/_3 \times 9$, or: $^1/_3 \times {^9}/_1$

Then perform the multiplication, cancelling where possible: $^1/_{\cancel{3}}{_1} \times {^3}\cancel{9}/_1 = {^3}/_1 = 3$

46

Example (v)

Find $^1/_3$ of $^5/_8$.

You carry out exactly the same procedure when you are finding a fraction of a fraction.

First set the problem out as a simple multiplication sum: $^3/_{10}$ x $^5/_8$.

Then perform the multiplication, cancelling where possible: $^3/_{\cancel{10}\,2}$ x $^{1}\cancel{5}/_8$ = $^3/_{16}$

Exercise 27

Calculate the following fractions of numbers:

(1) $^1/_3$ of 12   (2) $^5/_6$ of 36   (3) $^{11}/_{12}$ of 144

(4) $^2/_3$ of $^1/_2$ (5) $^5/_6$ of $^3/_{10}$ (6) $^2/_3$ of $^3/_8$

(7) $^1/_4$ of $^2/_5$ (8) $^5/_8$ of $^2/_3$

There is a short way to work out some of these fractions of questions. If you are finding *one* third, or *one* half or *one* tenth and so on, you can simply divide the second number by the bottom half of the fraction:

$^1/_3$ of 12 = 12 ÷ 3 = 4.

RULES FOR CANCELLING

We have seen how important cancelling is in many calculations involving fractions, so it is worthwhile learning the following rules, and the diagrams which will help you to remember them:

(1)   You can cancel any single fraction by dividing the top line (numerator) and bottom line (denominator) by the same number.

(2)   In multiplication sums you can cancel diagonally across the multiplication sign.

(3)   You must never cancel diagonally in addition or subtraction sums.

(4)   You must not cancel diagonally in division sums, until you have turned the fraction upside down and changed the sign to multiply.

(5)   Cancelling always involves one figure from the bottom line and one figure from the top line. You cannot cancel on the same line (such as cancelling two numerators, or two denominators).

It is normal procedure to cancel any single fractions, and ensure that they are reduced to their lowest terms first before you try to carry out any diagonal cancellations.

It may help you to remember these diagrams for the procedure for cancellation:

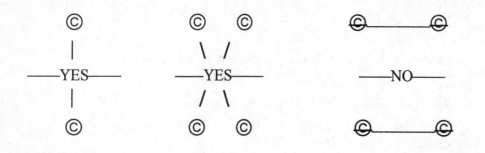

The first sign shows the simple cancellation of the top and bottom line of the same fraction. This means you divide the numerator and denominator by the same number.

The second sign shows the cancellation of two fractions in a multiplication diagonally, with the numerator of one and the denominator of the other cancelled, or both numerators and both denominators cancelled diagonally.

The third sign shows what you cannot do: cancel the two numerators with each other, or the two denominators with each other.

You can also remember these:

$+$ ⓒ   No cancelling diagonally

$-$ ⓒ   No cancelling diagonally

$\div$ ⓒ   No cancelling diagonally until you have turned the second fraction upside down.

X   ⓒ   Cancel diagonally.

Exercise 28   Revision of the Four Rules of Fractions

Carry out the following calculations involving fractions, making sure that you first perform any cancelling which can be done:

(1) $\frac{5}{6} + \frac{3}{5}$ (2) $3\frac{5}{6} + 6\frac{1}{4}$ (3) $\frac{18}{24} - \frac{3}{6}$

(4) $6\frac{2}{3} - 3\frac{7}{8}$ (5) $\frac{44}{63} \times \frac{9}{11}$ (6) $6\frac{2}{3} \times 4\frac{8}{10}$

(7) $\frac{3}{4} \div \frac{6}{16}$ (8) $5\frac{3}{5} \div 6\frac{3}{10}$ (9) $2\frac{7}{10} \div \frac{9}{20}$

(10) $\frac{5}{6}$ of $\frac{6}{5}$ (11) $\frac{1}{12}$ of 132

(12)   Find two thirds of the sum of one and a quarter and three and three eighths.

METRIC MEASURES

The metric system is a system of measurements for length, weight and capacity, which is based on the decimal system, and therefore operates in units of tens, and tenths.

Each level in the table of units has a special name in the metric system:

KILO..... = 1000 of   **k**

       HECTO..... = 100 of   **h**

            DEKA... = 10 of   **de**

                   THE MAIN UNIT OF MEASUREMENT

            DECI.... = $^1/_{10}$ of   **d**

       CENTI.... = $^1/_{100}$ of   **c**

MILLI.... = $^1/_{1000}$ of   **m**

You need to learn the units of measurement that we employ in the metric system.

Length

mm.	cm.	dm.	m.	dem.	hm.	km.
millimetre	centimetre	decimetre	METRE	dekametre	hectometre	kilometre
x 10 =	x 10 =	x 10 =	x 10 =	x 10 =	x 10 =	

If you read along this line you will see that 10 millimetres equal one centimetre, and ten centimetres equal one decimetre and so on.

The normal abbreviations for the units have been shown above.

The main unit on which all the others are based when measuring length is the **metre**.

Of the above units of measurement only four are in common use:
                millimetre; centimetre; metre; kilometre.

Learn this table for these four common measurement units:

10 millimetres = 1 centimetre   *100 centimetres = 1 metre* *1 000 metres = 1 kilometre.*

Weight

mg.	cg.	dg.	g.	deg.	hg.	kg.
milligram	centigram	decigram	GRAM	dekagram	hectogram	kilogram
x 10 =	x 10 =	x 10 =	x 10 =	x 10 =	x 10 =	

Once again, if you read along this line you will see that 10 milligrams equal one centigram, and ten centigrams equal one decigram and so on.

The normal abbreviations for the units have been shown above.

The main unit on which all the others are based when measuring length is the **gram**.

Of the above units of measurement only three are in common use:

milligram; gram; kilogram.

Learn this table for these three common measurement units:

1000 milligrams = 1 gram   *1000 grams = 1 kilogram.*

A kilogram is generally known simply as a *kilo*. 1 000 kilograms is known as a *metric tonne*.

Capacity

Capacity is the amount of liquid that something contains.

ml.	cl.	dl.	l.	del.	hl.	kl.
millilitre	centilitre	decilitre	LITRE	dekalitre	hectolitre	kilolitre
x 10 =	x 10 =	x 10 =	x 10 =	x 10 =	x 10 =	

Once again, if you read along this line you will see that 10 millilitres equal one centilitre, and ten centilitres equal one decilitre and so on.

The normal abbreviations for the units have been shown above.

The main unit on which all the others are based when measuring capacity is the **litre**.

Of the above units of measurement only two are in common use: millilitre; litre.
(However, decilitre and kilolitre are also occasionally employed, so be ready for them.)

Learn the equivalents for the two common measurement units: *1000 millilitres = 1 litre.*

Because the abbreviation l. can easily be confused with the number 1, it is often shown instead as a hand-written l, like this: *l.*

CONVERSION OF UNITS

The important things to remember are the 3 tables of equivalents given on the preceding two pages:

10 millimetres = 1 centimetre   *100 centimetres = 1 metre   1 000 metres = 1 kilometre.*
1000 milligrams = 1 gram   *1000 grams = 1 kilogram.*
1000 millilitres =   1 litre.

These equivalents will show you how to do the conversion.

If you are converting a smaller unit into a larger one, divide by the number given above.
If you are converting a larger unit into a smaller unit, multiply by the number given above.

Check the following cases, to make sure you understand:
 If you are converting centimetres into metres (smaller into larger) you divide by 100.
 If you are converting kilograms into grams (larger into smaller) you multiply by 1 000.
 If you are converting millilitres into litres (smaller into larger) you divide by 1 000.
 If you are converting metres into millimetres (larger into smaller) you multiply by 1 000.

(Notice this last case: 10 mm. in 1 cm. and 100 cm. in 1 m.; 10 x 100 = 1 000. You should, however, know by the prefix *milli-* that there are a thousand of these divisions in the main unit, the metre.)

Examples :

(a)   Convert 342 millimetres into metres.
    Divide by 1 000, so move the digits three places to the left across the decimal point.
    (You need to insert a decimal point after the figure when dividing.)
    3 420 mm. = 3.42 m.

(b)   Convert 7.8 metres into centimetres.
    Multiply by 100, so move the digits two places to the right across the decimal point.
    (You need to insert a zero in the vacant units column.)
    7.8 m. = 780 cm.

(c)   Convert 17 438 millilitres into litres.
    Divide by 1 000, so move the digits three places to the left across the decimal point.
    17 348 ml. = 17.349 *l*.

(d)   Convert 13.5 grams into milligrams.
    Multiply by 1 000, so move the digits three places to the right across the decimal point.
    13.5 g. = 13 500 mg.

When you are given measurements in vulgar fractions (such as *two and three quarter kilometres*), it will be necessary to convert them into decimal fractions for conversion.

It may help you to know that a kilometre is $\frac{5}{8}$ of a mile, a kilogram is rather less than two pounds, and a litre is rather less than two pints in the old units.

Exercise 29

(1)   Use your ruler to draw lines of the following lengths:
       (a)   3 cm.   (b)   7.5 cm.   (c)   4.25 cm.
       Measure the lines again in millimetres.
(2)   Change into metres:
       (a)   1 km.   (b)   0.55 km.   (c)   one and a half kilometres
(3)   Write the equivalents of the following in centimetres:
       (a)   132 m.   (b)   1 320 m.   (c)   1.32 m.
(4)   Write the equivalents of the above three measurements, in kilometres.
(5)   Change the following into grams:
       (a)   4 kg.   (b)   0.3 kg.   (c)   half a kilo.
       (d)   0.07 kg.   (e)   2 459 mg.   (f)   376 mg.
(6)   Change the following into kilograms:
       (a)   5 000 g.   (b)   6 750 g.   (c)   72 g.
       (d)   3 g.   (e)   12 349 mg.   (f)   1 000 000 mg.
(7)   Change into litres:
       (a)   4 700 ml.   (b)   629 ml.   (c)   30 ml.
(8)   Change into millilitres:
       (a)   0.03 ℓ.   (b)   3.6 ℓ.   (c)   three quarters of a litre

THE FOUR RULES OF METRIC MEASURES

The first thing to remember is that metric measurements move from one unit to the next in groups of TEN, just the same as the ordinary decimal system.

However, you will have noticed that many of the metric measurements are not in common use. So, for example, in measuring weight we really only use milligrams, grams and kilograms, and even milligrams are only used rarely, and for very small weights indeed.

Calculations involving the measurements in common use only often mean that for borrowing and carrying, we are not dealing in tens, but in hundreds or thousands.

Once again, you need the conversion table, so once again, here it is, but in a form that tells you the values of the units for carrying, and for borrowing and paying back:

millimetres   ⇐10⇒   *centimetre*
centimetres   ⇐100⇒   *metre*
millimetres   ⇐1 000⇒   *metre*
metres   ⇐1 000⇒   *kilometre*
milligrams   ⇐1 000⇒   *gram*
grams   ⇐1 000⇒   *kilogram.*
millilitres   ⇐1 000⇒   *litre*

It is sensible to learn the above form of this table for all your work with metric units.

The following examples should give you an idea of how to do calculations involving metric measures.

Example (a) Addition

```
km.        m.
18        716
 4        819  +
────────────────
23        535
────────────────
 1
```

In this example when we add up the first column (the equivalent of adding the 'units') we get a total of 1 535. But that is 1 535 metres. We check back to our table and discover that there are 1 000 metres in one kilometre. So every *thousand* metres must be carried to the next column as *one* kilometre. So we carry the thousand and have 535 left in the answer space.

Example (b) Subtraction

```
kg.         g.
 6        1000
 7          41        The figure on the top line in the grams column
 3         725   -    is now 1000 + 41 = 1041 grams.
────────────────
 3         316
────────────────
```

In this example, we cannot subtract 725 grams from 41 grams, so we have to borrow from the kilograms column. We consult our table again, and we find that there are a thousand grams in a kilogram. So when we borrow *one* kilogram from the kg. column, it appears as a *thousand* grams in the g. column.
We can now subtract 725 from 1041 (1000 + 41 = 1041). And we remember to reduce the kg. column by the one kg. which we borrowed.

Example (c) Multiplication

```
       l.        ml.
       10        235
 x                15
────────────────────
       51        175
        1        1 2
       12        350
        2
────────────────────
       63        525
────────────────────
                  1
```

53

This is an example of long multiplication, and is quite hard. But all you have to remember is to proceed as for an ordinary long multiplication, except that you must also check the metric units used for your carrying. So in this case we multiply the ml. column by the five first. The result is 1175 ml. There are a thousand millilitres in a litre, so we carry the thousand millilitres into the column as 1 litre, and write down the remaining 175 ml. in the answer. Then we multiply the litres by the five, remembering to add on the one we have carried.

This is a long multiplication, so after we have multiplied by the units, we must multiply by the tens. Before doing so, remember to insert a zero. This goes on the right hand side as in a normal long multiplication, so it belongs in the millilitres column (in the second row of the answer calculation). Then we multiply the 235 by one. Because of the zero we have already inserted, the result is: 2350 ml. We check the table, find that a thousand millilitres make a litre, and since we have two thousand millilitres we carry two over to the litres column, and write down the 350 ml. remaining in the millilitres column. Then we multiply the ten litres by one, and remember to add on the two we have carried.

Finally we add together the two rows of our working - just as in a normal long multiplication - and the result is the answer to our multiplication sum. In this example the millilitres did not add up to one thousand or more, so there was nothing to carry to the litres column in the final addition.

Example (d) Division

Divide 4 m. 80 cm. by 8.

```
           m.          cm.
           0           60
        _____
    8 ) 4            ⁴80
```

This is a short division and so is quite easy. You can see that eight will not divide into the four into the metres column, so the next job is to convert the 4 m. into centimetres. There are a hundred centimetres in a metre, so you have four hundred to carry across to the centimetres column. There are already 80 cm. there, so you can conveniently write the 4 (for four hundred) in front of the 80. Then you can divide the 480 by eight very easily, and the result: 60 can be written in the answer space.

Example (e) Long Division

```
           m.          mm.
           1           544
        _____
   13 ) 20            98
         13
       _____
          7   ⇒       7000   +
                      7098              0544
                      7098          13)7098
       _____                         7098
                         0
```

Example (e) is harder because it is long division. You have to divide 20 m. 98 mm. by 13.
Start by dividing the metres column. Twenty divided by 13 is one, with 7 remaining. The seven must be converted into millimetres, and since there are a thousand millimetres in a metre, it becomes 7 000 mm. when we carry it across into the millimetres column. Then we have to add on the 98 mm. already there, making a total of 7098 mm. altogether. This must then be divided by the 13 as well.

The working is only shown in a short form next to the example itself on page 54, but here it is in full, in case you are not sure how the result was achieved:

```
   0546          13    13
13)7098           5 x   4 x
   65            65    52
   59
   52            13
   78             6 x
   78            78
    0
```

When you get questions in which different metric measurements are mixed up, you will find it easiest to convert all the measures to a single unit or set of units before carrying out your calculation. Remember that units can often be expressed as decimal fractions of other units. Thus, 1 metre 28 centimetres could appear as 1.28 m., while 3.09 kilograms could be written as 3 kg. 90 g. Check the table if you are not sure how many units are involved in the conversion, so that you get the decimal point in the correct place.

Exercise 30

Set out correctly these calculations involving metric measures, and work them out:

1. 8 m. 19 mm. - 3 m. 45 mm.   2. 12 m. 23 cm. + 9 m. 77 cm.
3. 12 km. 941 m. + 873 m.   4. 13 kg. 7 g. - 12 kg. 875 g.
5. 4 cm. 9 mm. x 7   6. 7 kl. 60 l. ÷ 4   7. 5 l. 68 ml. ÷ 8
8. 6 kg. 453 g. x 16   9. 47 g. 82 mg. ÷ 21   10. 17 cm. 5 mm. ÷ 25

The following exercises also deal with metric measures, but they are given in problem form, and you must
first work out which operation you need to use to calculate the result.

Exercise 30 A   Problems (Length) (For A.T. 2 Levels 4 to 6)

1. By how many *millimetres* is 7.5 cm. greater than 4.8 cm. ?
2. A metal bar is 59 cm. long. What length would 19 of these bars placed end to end measure ? Give your answer in metres.
3. A runner in a 5 000 metre race gave up after he had run $^2/_5$ of the race. How far (in metres) had he still to run ?
4. A rope 36 m. 80 cm. long is cut into 8 equal pieces. How long is each piece:
    (a) in metres; (b) in centimetres ?
5. A tailor cut three separate lengths from a 50 metre roll of material. The first length he cut was 3.8 m., the second was 6.25 m. and the third was 4.7 m. How much material was left on the roll ?

Exercise 30 B   Problems (Weight) (For A.T. 2 Levels 4 to 6)

1.   By how many *milligrams* is 9.803 g. greater than 8.703 g. ?

2.   A girl buys twenty-eight 250 g. packets of assorted sweets to give to each of her friends who are attending her birthday party. What is the total weight of the sweets she buys in kilograms ?

3.   How many milligrams are there in $^1/_{20}$ of a kilogram ?

4.   A builders' merchant has 3 tonnes* of sand in stock. He sells the sand in 28 kg bags. In one day he sells 30 of these bags.
    (a)   How much sand does he sell by weight ?
    (b)   How much sand by weight does he have left ?
    (c)   How many 28 kg bags can he put the remaining sand into ?

5.   Into a box which weighs 200 g. when empty are packed twelve equal packages.

    The total weight of the box and the packages is $6^1/_2$ kg. What is the weight of each of the twelve packages ?

(* A tonne is 1 000 kilograms.)

Exercise 30 C   Problems (Capacity) (For A.T. 2 Levels 4 to 6)

1.   How many millilitres are there in seven eighths of a litre ?

2.   How many 250 ml. bottles can be filled from an 8 litre container ?

3.   3.2 litres of milk are shared equally among 16 children. How many millilitres of milk did each child get ?

4.   A shop sold 13 two litre bottles of lemonade, 27 one litre bottles, 36 half litre bottles, and fourteen 250 ml. bottles. How many *litres* of lemonade did the shop sell ?

5.   In a laboratory was a bottle containing 3.375 litres of liquid chemical. 1 235 ml. of liquid were poured out of a bottle for use. Only 860 ml. were needed, so the rest was returned to the bottle. How much did the bottle then contain ?

MONEY

The British system of money is based on decimal currency, and has the pound as its base unit.

The pound is written with this sign: *£* in front.

The only sub unit is the penny (plural: pence). There are 100 pence in one pound.

A decimal point is used to separate pounds from pence, so a sum of pounds and pence will be written like these examples: £ 23.74,   £ 171.90,   £ 2.08

When a sum of pence is written, it can be done in the same way, with a zero in the pounds place, like this: £ 0.87,   £ 0.08.
Alternatively it can be written as a simple figure followed by the abbreviation: **p.** ,
like this: 87 p.,   8 p.

There is only one table you need to learn for converting pence into pounds or pounds into pence:
pounds   *⇐100⇒*   *pence*

Even this is not really necessary, as all calculations involving pounds and pence can be carried out in exactly the same way as any other decimal calculations, just as you have learnt in Topic Four (page 17).

These calculations should normally be set out in pounds, and you must remember to show the pounds sign (or occasionally the pence sign) in your answer.

You can see how the four rules of money operate in the following examples:

Example (a)   Addition

Find the sum of: Three pounds ninety, £8.54 and Twelve pounds 72 p.

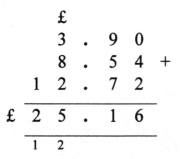

(Notice the various ways in which we can write and say a figure involving pounds and pence.)

Example (b)   Subtraction

What is the difference between £163.28 and £284.32

```
            £
    2   8   4  .  ²3 ¹2
    1   6   3  .   2   8  -
   _____
£   1   2   1  .   0   4
   _____
```

Example (c)   Multiplication

Multiply £ 91.32 by 24

```
            £
        9   1  .  3   2
        x         2   4
       _____
        3   6   5   2   8
                    ¹
    1   8   2   6   4   0
    ¹
   _____
    2   1   9   1   6   8
   _____
    ¹           ¹
```

£   2   1   9   1 . 6   8

Notice that, as in any multiplication of decimals, we ignore the decimal points until the end, and then insert them on the basis of the number of places of decimals in the original figures being multiplied. So here we have the two places of decimals indicated by the figures after the point (the pence).

Example (d)   Division

Divide £ 72.32 by 16.

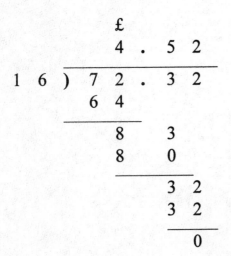

```
                £
                4  .  5   2
            _____
    1   6  )  7   2  .  3   2
              6   4
            _____
                  8   3
                  8   0
                _____
                      3   2
                      3   2
                    _____
                          0
```

58

As you can see, we treat the calculation exactly like a division of decimals. If your answer goes on beyond two places of decimals (which in money would indicate fractions of a penny), you can ignore these figures, and simply calculate to two decimal places.

Now go on to the two exercises. In the second one (31 A) you will need to work out which rule(s) you need to use to get to the answer.

Exercise 31

Set out correctly and then work out the following:

1. Increase £ 296.58 by £ 98.77.   2.   Find the sum of: £ 48.22, £ 123.59 and £ 1 093.96

3. Decrease £ 962.44 by £ 872.86   4.   By how much is £ 193.72 more than £ 67.98 ?

5. To the difference between £ 152.70 and £ 111.49 add £ 92.87.

6. Multiply £ 204.23 by 9.   7.   What is 67 times £ 31.95 ?

8. Divide £ 22.54 by 7.   9.   Share £ 36.08 between eight people equally.

10. What is (a) $\frac{1}{10}$ and (b) $\frac{1}{100}$ of £ 39 ?

Exercise 31 A   Problems

1. Achmed is given an increase of £ 11.98 on his weekly pay. Before the increase he earned £ 162.74 per week. What does he get after the increase ?

2. Jack wins £ 1 755.95 on the pools. He has to share this equally with another four friends. How much does each of them get ?

3. A man has £ 2 841.74 in the bank. From this he has to pay an electricity bill of £ 93.77, and a gas bill of £ 64.22. After paying the bills, how much does he have left in the bank ?

4. Find the total cost of 172 articles at 19p. each.

5. In one week a shopkeeper receives: £ 3 942.01 in cash; £ 2 641.79 in credit card payments; and one and a half times the sum of both in payments by cheque. What are his total receipts ?

6. The total price of 241 identical items was £ 103.63. How much did each item cost ?

7. Four hundred people in a factory formed a syndicate, which won a national lottery prize. Each person received an equal share of £ 4 000. How much was the total prize ?

8. How many bars of chocolate costing 23 pence each can you buy for £11.96 ?

PERIMETER

The perimeter of a shape is the distance all round its edge or border.

Depending on the size of the shape it can be measured in:
    millimetres (mm..), centimetres (cm.), metres (m.) or kilometres (km.)

There are simple ways of working out the perimeter of regular shapes, like squares and rectangles.

A **square** is a regular shape in which all the sides are of equal length.

A **rectangle** is a regular shape in which opposite sides are of equal length.
(You may also know that all the angles in squares and rectangles are right angles, which means that each side is vertical or horizontal to the next).

Example 1 - A rectangle

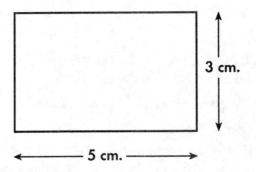

Only two of the sides have been marked with a measurement on this diagram of a rectangle. But in fact we know that the opposite sides to the marked ones have the same measurements. So there are two sides of 3 cm. and two sides of 5 cm.

The perimeter (the distance round the edge) is therefore: 5 cm. + 5 cm. + 3 cm. + 3 cm. = 16 cm.

There is a shorter way of doing this: (5 cm. + 3 cm.) x 2 = 8 cm. x 2 = 16 cm.

What this means is that we add the two side lengths we have been given, and then multiply the result by two, since we know each side length occurs twice.

In the case of a square, all the side lengths are the same. So we only need to be told one of them. We must then multiply the length of the one side we are given by four, to have all four sides, and the complete measurement for the perimeter.

So in a square of side 6 cm., we know we have four sides, so we multiply the 6 cm. by four, and get the complete perimeter measurement as 24 cm.

If you are told certain information about a shape, you can often work out other information.

So if you know only one side of a square, you can work out its perimeter at once: multiply by 4.

In the same way if you are told a square's perimeter, you can work out the length of each of the sides by reversing the process: divide by 4.

If you know one side of a rectangle, and its perimeter, you can work out the other side:
Double the measurement for the side you have (because there are two sides of that length).
Subtract the result from the perimeter: the result is the combined length of the remaining sides.
Divide the result by two to get the length of each of the remaining sides.

Sometimes you may be given measurements involving decimal quantities or fractions. In these cases you will have to use your knowledge of decimals and fractions in the calculation.

Sometimes you may be given mixtures of units (for example metres and centimetres). In this case use the unit which seems the most convenient. Depending on the size of the shape it can be measured in: millimetres (mm.), centimetres (cm.), metres (m.) or kilometres (km.). If the question you have been asked tells you to give your answer in a particular measurement, then it may well be easiest to use that unit throughout. If you are not told, you must decide which you prefer.

Exercise 32

1. Find the perimeter of a rectangle 8 m. by 7 m.
2. Find the perimeter of a square of side 11.5 cm.
3. Find the perimeter of a rectangle 11.5 mm. by 9.5 mm.
4. Find the perimeter of a rectangle 150 mm. by 6.5 cm.
5. The perimeter of a square is 80 cm. Find the length of each side.
6. The perimeter of a rectangle is 30 m. One side is 10 m. long. Write down the lengths of each of the other three sides.
7. A square has a perimeter of exactly on metre. How many millimetres long is each side ?
8. In a rectangle, two sides are each 34 mm. long. If the perimeter of the rectangle is 20.4 cm., how long is each of the other sides ?
9. In a rectangle of perimeter 160 mm., if you are told that one side is 4 cm. long, what can you work out about the nature of the particular rectangle ?
10. Two adjacent (= touching) sides of a rectangle together measure 219 mm.
    What is the perimeter of the rectangle ?
    Is it possible to work out the length of the individual sides of the rectangle ?
11. The perimeter of a rectangle is 276 mm. Its length is exactly twice its width.
    Find: (a)   each of the two longer sides   (b)   each of the two shorter sides.
12. A rectangle measuring 3 cm. by 8 cm. is attached end on to a square of side 3 cm.
    What is the total perimeter of the rectangle created in this way ?
    (Be careful, this is a trick question ! Think what happens to both sides where the join occurs. Are they still part of the perimeter ?)

When you have to work out the perimeter of an irregular shape (squares and rectangles are regular shapes), you have no choice but to add together all the different sides. In the following example, the measurements have been given in a mixture of units - centimetres and millimetres. They have been noted down in turn in the column underneath, and all have been converted into centimetres. For practice you should prepare a similar table, with all the measurements, and the perimeter, shown in millimetres.

Example (2)

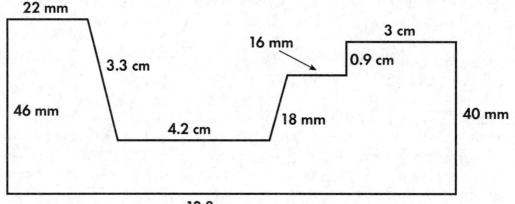

Measurements in centimetres (starting at the top left hand corner and working clockwise):

          2.2 cm.
          3.3 cm.
          4.2 cm.
          1.8 cm.
          1.6 cm.
          0.9 cm.
          3.0 cm.
          4.0 cm.
         12.3 cm.
          4.6 cm.
          _____
Perimeter =   37.9 cm
          _____

AREA

The area of a shape is the surface contained inside its perimeter.

The perimeter, as you will remember from the last topic, is the edge of a shape, and to measure it, you add together all the sides. We looked at easy ways to find the perimeter of squares and rectangles. Finding the area of a square or rectangle is just as easy as finding its perimeter.

Area is measured by dividing the shape into equal squares and then counting them. We could find the area of a shape by actually drawing the squares in across its surface, but you will see from the following examples that there is a short-cut we can use.

Example 1

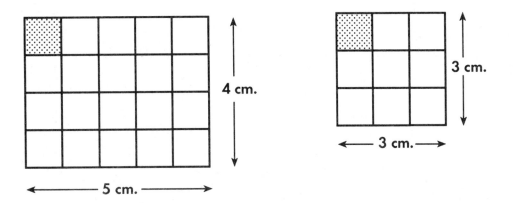

Look carefully at the first of the two shapes. As you can see it is a rectangle, of side 5 cm. by 4 cm.
It has been divided up into 20 separate squares, each with side 1 cm.
The first of these 1 cm. squares has been shaded.
Instead of speaking of 1 cm. squares, we usually speak of square centimetres.
This is the abbreviation for square centimetres : cm^2.
Since this shape has 20 squares of 1 cm., its **area** is 20 square centimetres, or 20 **cm²**.

Now look at the second shape. As you can see it is a square of side 3 cm.
It has also been divided up into separate 1 cm. squares, with the first shaded.
Altogether it contains 9 one centimetre squares. So its area is 9 **cm²**.

If you look at these figures you should realise two things:

Firstly: Area is measured in square units
Secondly: The area of a rectangle is the length times the width - with square units.

So for the rectangle above we have: 4 cm. x   5 cm. = 20 **cm²**.
For the square: 3 cm. x   3 cm. = 9 **cm²**.
(Since all the sides in a square are equal, you simply have to multiply one side by itself.)

The square units you will be likely to meet are the equivalents of the commonly used metric measures for length which we have already studied in Topic 8:

square millimetres: mm^2
square centimetres: cm^2
square metres: m^2
square kilometres: km^2

Always remember to write your answer with the square units clearly shown. In an examination, answers shown without the units, or with the incorrect units (such as cm. instead of cm^2) may be marked wrong.

Learn the simple formula for working out area:

$$AREA \quad = \quad LENGTH \quad X \quad WIDTH$$

Use the following method of layout for calculations where you have to find the area of a rectangle:

Example (2)

Find the area of a rectangle 8 cm. long and 4 cm. wide.

$$A = L \text{ x } W \text{ units}^2$$
$$A = 8 \text{ x } 4 \text{ cm}^2$$
$$A = 32 \text{ cm}^2$$

If you get a problem where you know the area and one side of a rectangle, you can calculate the unknown side, by dividing the area by the side:

Example (3)

Find the length of a rectangle where the width is 7 cm. long and the area is 63 cm^2 .

$$L = A \div W \text{ units.}$$
$$L = 63 \div 7 \text{ cm.}$$
$$L = 32 \text{ cm.}$$

This time you have to remember that your result will be in linear measure, not square measure.

The same method exactly can of course be used if you know the length but not the width.

To find the area of a square, since all the sides are the same length, you multiply the measurement of any side by itself.
If you know the area of a square, you can find out the length of its sides by trying to calculate what two numbers multiplied together give you the exact figure for the area.
So, for example, if you know the area of a square is 25 cm^2 , you can quickly see that 5 x 5 = 25, so each of the sides measures 5 cm.

Exercise 33

(1)   Find the area of rectangles of the following measurements:

(a)   15 cm. by 6 cm.   (b)   200 mm. by 100 mm.   (c)   14 m. by 8 m.
(d)   18 cm. by 9 mm.   (e)   4 m. by 97 cm.   (f)   8.5 m. by 2 000 mm.

(2)   Find the area of squares of the following side:

(a)   9.3 cm. (answer in mm.)   (b)   0.76 m. (answer in m.)   (c)   18 km.

(3)   Find the length or width of the following rectangles:

(a)   area 56 m^2 , length 8 m.   (b)   area 81 cm^2 , length 9 cm.
(c)   area 108 mm^2 , width 9 mm   (d)   area 36 cm^2 , width 40 mm.

(4)   Copy the following table, and fill in the missing measurements:

	AREA	LENGTH	WIDTH
(a)	42 cm^2	7 cm.	....
(b)	54 cm^2	....	6 cm.
(c)	....	13 cm.	11 cm.
(d)	144 mm^2	1.2 cm.	....
(e)	27.5 m^2	....	5 m.
(f)	....	8.5 m.	750 mm.

Exercise 33 A   Problems (For Level 3, AT 5)

(1)   A farmer purchases two rectangular fields. One measures 214 m. by 730 m. The other measures 700 m. by 850 m. What is the total area of the land he purchases ?

(2)   How many house plots each measuring 12m. by 10 m. can be fitted into a rectangular strip of land of area 480 m^2 ?

(3)   On one street there are four houses. Their frontages on the street are: 15 m., 10 m., 12 m. and 13 m. respectively. The back gardens of these houses all end at a wall along the same straight line. The total area of the four houses and their gardens is 810 m^2 .
   (a)   What is the length of the land occupied by each house and garden, from street to wall ?
   (b)   Calculate the area of each separate house plot.

(4)   In a garden 12 m. long and 11 m. wide, the flower beds occupy 33 m^2 , and the patio occupies another 50 m^2 . The rest of the garden is occupied by a square lawn.
   What is the length of each side of the lawn ?

(5)   A lawn is 22 metres long and 7 metres wide. All the way round the outside of it is a path 3.5 metres wide. What is the area of the path ?

65

VOLUME

Volume is the space taken up by a solid figure or object.

We measure the volume of a solid figure by seeing how many cubic units it contains.

Volume works on the same principle as area. To find the area of a shape, we had to find how many square units it contained.

We are learning to measure the area of two regular solids:
The cube   - *a square box*
The cuboid   - *a rectangular box.*

To find the volume of a figure, we have to find how many cubic units it contains. We have to divide the figure into equal cubes, and then count them. We could actually do this, but there is a shorter method, as there is for area. Look at the following diagram to see how it works.

Example 1

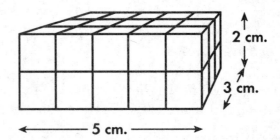

This diagram shows a cuboid, divided up into 1 cm. cubes.

Two layers of one centimetre cubes fit into the shape in the diagram. Each layer consists of four times three cubes. Therefore the total number of 1 cm. cubes which fit into the shape is: 5 x 3 x 2 = 30. Instead of speaking of 1 cm. cubes, we usually speak of cubic centimetres.

The abbreviation for square centimetres is: cm^3.

Since this shape has 30 cubes of 1 cm., its **volume** is 30 cubic centimetres, or 30 cm^3.

So we can now state:

Firstly: Volume is measured in cubic units
Secondly: The volume of a cuboid is the length times the breadth times the height - in cubic units.

So for the cuboid above we have: 5 cm. x   3 cm. x 2 cm. = 30 cm^3.

The cubic units you will be likely to meet are the equivalents of the commonly used metric measures for length , and of course the square measures which we have just studied in Topic 11:

cubic millimetres: mm^3
cubic centimetres: cm^3
cubic metres: m^3

Note: You may also come across the old abbreviation for cubic centimetres: **cc.**
This is very often used for stating the capacity of engines.

Here is another interesting and useful table by which different metric measurements are linked:

1 000 cm^3 (of water) =
          1 000 ml. (1 litre) (of water) =
                    1 000 g. (1 kilogram) (of water)

Always remember to write your answer with the cubic units clearly shown. In an examination, answers shown without the units, or with the incorrect units (such as cm. instead of cm^3) may be marked wrong.

Learn the simple formula for working out volume:

$$\text{VOLUME} \quad = \quad \text{LENGTH} \quad X \quad \text{BREADTH} \quad X \quad \text{HEIGHT}$$

When you are dealing with a cube, all the sides, length, breadth and height are the same, so you are simply multiplying the same number three times.

It is very important that you do not mix units in your calculations, so if the question mixes units, make sure you convert them all to the most convenient, or to the unit called for in the answer.

Use the following method of layout for calculations where you have to find the area of a cuboid:

Example (2)

Find the volume of a cuboid 4 m. long and 80 cm. wide and 2.5 metres high.

All the units must be the same before we start, so if we are going to work in metres and cubic metres, then we need to convert 80 cm. into metres (0.8 metres).

$$V = L \times B \times H \text{ units}^3.$$
$$V = 4 \times 0.8 \times 2.5 \text{ } m^3.$$
$$V = 8 \text{ } m^3.$$

Alternatively you could work it out in cubic centimetres:

$$V = 400 \times 80 \times 250 = 800\,000 \text{ } cm^3.$$

In order to avoid confusingly large numbers of zeros, you may well prefer to work in larger units and decimal fractions of those units, as in the first method in this example.

If you get a problem where you know the volume and any two sides of a cuboid, you can calculate the unknown side, by multiplying the two known sides lengths together, and dividing the volume by the product of the multiplication:

Example (3)

Find the width of a cuboid where the length is 7 cm., the height is 3 cm. and the volume is 84 cm^3 .

$$W \ = \ A \div (L \times H) \text{ units.}$$
$$W \ = \ 84 \div (7 \times 3) \text{ cm.}$$
$$W \ = \ 84 \div 21 \text{ cm.}$$
$$W \ = \ 4 \text{ cm.}$$

This time you have to remember that your result will be in linear measure, not square measure.

The same method exactly can of course be used if you know the area and the other two side measurements, and are trying to find the length or the height .

If you know the volume of a square, you can find out the length of its sides by trying to calculate what three identical numbers multiplied together give you the exact figure for the volume.
So, for example, if you know the area of a square is 27 cm^3 , you can probably quickly see that :
3 x 3 x 3 = 27, so each of the sides measures 3 cm.

Exercise 34

(1)   Find the volume of cuboids of the following measurements:

(a)   3 cm. x 5 cm. x 1 cm.   (b)   4 cm. x 9 mm. x 3 cm.
(c)   1 m. x 30 cm. x 9 mm.

(2)   Find the volume of cubes of the following side:

(a)   2.3 cm.   (b)   0.7 cm. (answer in mm^3.)   (c)   18 m.

(3)   Find the height, length or width of the following cuboids:

(a)   volume 36 m^3; height 6 m.; width 2m.   (b)   volume 64 cm^3; length 4 cm.; width 4 cm.
(c)   volume 600 mm^3 ; height 5 mm. ; length 12 mm.

(4)   Copy the following table, and fill in the missing measurements:

	VOLUME	LENGTH	WIDTH	HEIGHT
(a)	....	10 cm.	3 cm.	5 cm.
(b)	....	6 m.	4 m.	5 m.
(c)	....	10 mm.	3 mm.	1 mm.
(d)	28 mm^3	7 mm.	....	2 mm.
(e)	630 cm^3	....	7 cm.	9 cm.
(f)	60 m^3	12 m.	5 m.	....

Exercise 34 A   Problems (For Level 3, AT 5)

(1)   How many cubic centimetres are contained in one cubic metre ?

(2)   A box is 10 cm. long and 6 cm. wide.
    (a)   What is the area of the bottom of the box ?
    (b)   How many 1 cm. cubes would be needed to cover the bottom of the box completely ?
    (c)   If the box is 14 cm. high, how many layers of cubes will fit inside it ?
    (d)   What is the volume of the box ?

(3)   A cubic bar of soap has a side of 500 mm. How many of these bars will fir inside a box with the dimensions: 3 m. by 2 m. by 1.5 m. ?

(4)   What would be the smallest volume required for a container to take twelve dozen chocolate bars each 12 cm. long, 4 cm. wide and 1 cm. high ?

(5)   A box contains exactly 200 cartons measuring 7 cm. by 9 cm. by 3 cm. If 150 of these are taken out, what volume of space is created in the box ?

Exercise 34 B   Problems (For Level 3, AT 5 and 6)

For this exercise you need to know the table:
$1\ 000\ cm^3$ =   1 000 ml. (1 litre)   =   1 000 g. (1 kilogram).

1.   If $1\ 000\ cm^3$ of water takes up the same space as 1 litre of water, what space do 350 ml. of water take up ?

2.   A jug has a volume of $375\ cm^3$. What fraction of a litre of water can it hold ?

3.   A tank measures 3 m. by 1.5 m. by 2.5 m. How many litres of water will it hold ?

4.   An empty bottle weighs 300 g. What is its weight when it holds a litre of water ?

5.   A tank full of water weighs 14.725 kg. The empty tank weighs 2.85 kg.
What is the capacity of the tank in litres ?

6.   A container measures one metre by 80 centimetres by 160 millimetres.
    (a)   What is its capacity in litres ?
    (b)   What weight of water would it hold when completely filled ?

7.   A tank holds 1 200 litres of water when full. How many jugs, each holding 600 g. in weight of water, can be filled from the tank ?

8.   A room measures 16 m. long, 8 m. wide and 3.5 m. high. The area of the door, fireplace and window works out at $9\ m^2$ in total.
    (a)   Find the remaining area of the room (walls, floor and ceiling).
    (b)   Calculate the volume of the room.
    (c)   If a litre of paint covers $10\ cm^2$, how many litres of paint will be needed to paint the walls (excluding the door, fireplace and window) and the ceiling of the room ?

TIME

When we are doing problems involving time we have to learn the table of equivalent times.
You should know it already, but it is set out here, and if you do not know any part of it, learn it now:

60 seconds	*=*	*1 minute*
60 minutes	*=*	*1 hour*
24 hours	*=*	*1 day*
7 days	*=*	*1 week*
52 weeks	*=*	*1 year*
365 days	*=*	*1 year*

Because of these strange numbers, when we do calculations involving time, we have problems involving borrowing, paying back and carrying. You have already seen how this can be difficult in dealing with some of the metric measures - where, for example, it may often be a thousand of one unit equal another unit (1 000 mm. = 1 m. ; 1 000 ml. = 1 litre; 1 000 g. = 1 kg. etc.).

The following examples should give you an idea of how to do calculations involving time.

Example (a) Addition

Add: 9 weeks, 5 days; 18 weeks, 4 days; and 3 weeks, 6 days

weeks	days	
9	5	
18	4	
3	6	+
32	1	

2

In this example when we add up the first column (the equivalent of adding the 'units') we get a total of 15. But that is 15 days. We know that there are seven days in a week (not ten days). So every *seven* days must be carried to the next column as *one* week. We have two sets of seven days here, so that is 2 weeks to carry, and one day left over goes in the answer space.

We can then go on to the weeks column, and add that up, remembering to include the two weeks we have carried. So we have 32 weeks and one day as the final answer.

If you have a large number of days in your addition, and are not sure immediately how many weeks they make up, you should use the space beside the sum to do a division by seven. The answer to the division is the number of weeks, and the remainder (if any) is the number of days left over.

Example (b)   Subtraction

Subtract 7 hours, 34 minutes, 20 seconds from 19 hours, 15 minutes, 10 seconds.

hours	mins.	secs.
$^{18}\cancel{19}$	$^{14}\cancel{15}$	10
7	34	20
11	40	50

This time we have a calculation with three columns: hours minutes and seconds. Work through it just as if it was an ordinary hundreds, tens and units subtraction, except that the figure for what is borrowed will be different (in this example: 60 on both occasions when borrowing is needed).

We cannot subtract 20 seconds from ten seconds, so we have to borrow from the minutes column. We know there are sixty seconds in a minute, so when we borrow one minute, we have to write in 60 in the seconds column. So the top line of the seconds column now has the original 10 seconds, plus the sixty we have borrowed: 70 altogether. Now we can do the subtraction: 70 - 20 = 50. Fifty seconds goes into the answer space. And we remember to repay the one minute we borrowed, by reducing the 15 minutes on the top line to 14.

Once again, in the minutes column we have a subtraction that cannot be done (14 - 34). So once again we borrow, this time from the hours column. Once again the figure for the minutes is 60, as there are 60 minutes in one hour. So we have 60 plus the original 14 = 74 minutes, and 74 minus 34 is 40. We write the forty in the minutes column, and remember to reduce the top line of the hours column from 19 to 18.

Finally all we have to do is complete the subtraction of the hours column: 18 - 7 = 11.

The answer is: 11 hours   40 minutes   50 seconds.

Example (c) Multiplication

Multiply 12 days 6 hours 30 minutes by 4

days	hours	mins.
12	6	30
	x	4
49	26	0
1	2	

The first thing to do is multiply the minutes column. The result is 120 minutes. There are 60 minutes in an hour, so we have to see how many sixties there are in 120. The answer is exactly two - so we have two hours to carry, and no minutes left in the minutes column.

The next thing to do is multiply the hours column: 4 x 6 = 24 , plus the two we carried = 26. There are 24 hours in a day, so with 26 hours we have one complete day, and two hours over.

We carry the one day to the days column, and write the two hours in the answer space.

Finally we multiply the 12 days by four, and add on the one day we carried, giving a total of 49 days.

Example (d) Division

Divide 14 years. 34 weeks by 6.

```
          years          weeks
           2              23
        ─────────────────────────
   6   )  14        104   34
```

104 + 34	138 ÷ 6
= 138	= 23

First we divide six into the 14 years. Two sixes are twelve, so that goes in the answer space, and there are two over.

We now have to convert that two - which is two years - into weeks.
There are 52 weeks in one year. So in two years there are 52 x 2 = 104 weeks.

So we have to carry 104 over to the weeks column, and add it on to the 34 already there.
That gives us 138 weeks altogether.

We now divide 138 by 6, to get the result 23, which goes in the answer space.

Exercise 35

Work out these calculations involving the four rules for time:

1.   45 minutes + 3 hours 20 mins.   2.   17 mins. 45 secs. - 16 mins. 50 secs.

3.   17 days 12 hours 15 minutes + 113 days 12 hrs. 50 mins. + 48 hours.

4.   7 years 14 weeks 6 days - 5 years 28 weeks.

5.   13 hrs. 14 mins. 15 secs. x 4   6.   18 weeks 5 days x 12

7.   9 days 3 hrs. 20 mins ÷ 8   8.   6 years 35 days ÷ 5

TIME ON THE CLOCK

It is assumed that you can already tell the time. If you cannot, immediately ask your teacher to help you to do so. It is essential.

As you know each day, in normal use, is divided into two periods of twelve hours (which we generally describe as morning and afternoon). The twelve hours which start immediately after midnight and finish at noon are followed by the abbreviation: **a.m.** The twelve hours from noon to midnight are followed by the abbreviation **p.m.**

Timetables use the twenty-four hour clock, which starts immediately after midnight and continues through the day to the next midnight.

To convert times from the normal usage to the 24-hour clock:
    (a)   a.m. times stay the same (but omit the letters a.m.)
    (b)   p.m. times must be increased by 12 (and the letters p.m. omitted).

To convert times from the 24-hour clock to normal usage:
    (a)   If the time shown is less than 13, it remains the same (followed by the letters: a.m.).
    (b)   If the time shown is more than 13, reduce it by 12 (and add the letters: p.m.).

Minutes are not affected by the change, only hours.

Here is a diagram of the 12- and 24-hour clocks to show the equivalents.

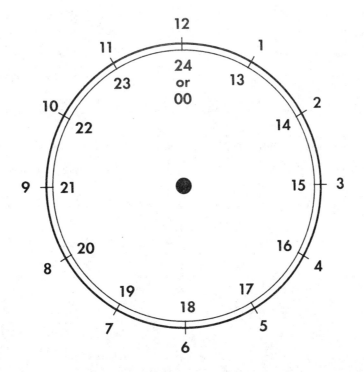

The most common calculations involving time are concerned with how long something takes. These are calculations which involve understanding the clock face, and working out the difference between two times, or adding an amount of time to the time shown on the clock.
It is generally easier to work out this sort of problem using the twenty-four hour clock.

Consider some of the uses of addition and subtraction of time:

Example (e)

We may want to find out what the time will be in, say, half an hour, or two hours.
In this case we need to add a period of time to a time on the clock.

The bus leaves in one and a half hour's time. It is now 11.40 a.m. What time does it leave ?

This is a simple addition:

hours	mins.	
11	40	⇐ time now
1	30	+
13	10	
1		

We now have the time the bus leaves - in the 24-hour clock. We can convert it to normal use by subtracting 12 hours from the answer, which gives us the time as: 1.30 p.m.

Example (f)

More commonly you will need to work out how much time is available (for carrying out a piece of work within a time limit for example), or how long you may have to wait (between now and tea-time, for example), or how long something takes (the journey to go on holiday, when you know the departure and arrival times, for example).

All these are simple subtractions. You have to take the start time away from the end time.

Subtractions are very complicated in normal time usage if you have to cross from a.m. to p.m. In such cases it is always far simpler to work in the 24-hour clock, and convert your result back if you need to.

A train departs at 8.30 in the morning, and arrives at 1.15 p.m. How long does the journey take ?

First convert the p.m. time into the 24-hour clock: 1.15 p.m. = 13.15.

	hours	mins.	
	$^{12}\cancel{13}$	$^{60}15$	⇐ end time
-	8	30	⇐ start time
	4	45	⇐ journey time

Notice that you have to borrow one hour (converted into sixty minutes) to do this subtraction.

Exercise 35 A

1. Convert the following into the twenty-four hour clock:
   (a) 3.15 p.m.   (b) 7.25 a.m.   (c) 12.20 a.m.   (d) 12.20 p.m.

2. Convert the following into the twelve-hour clock:
   (a) 09.30   (b) 17.55   (c) 20.12   (d) 00.17

3. How many minutes are there between the following times:
   (a) 3.15 p.m. and 4.25 p.m.   (b) 11.38 a.m. and 12.10 p.m.
   (c) 17.25 and 19.20   (d) 23.50 and 00.10

4. How many hours and minutes are there between the following times:
   (a) 3.17 p.m. and 7.30 p.m.   (b) 9.15 a.m. and 3.20 p.m.
   (c) 00.20 and 13.15   (d) 12.45 a.m. and 1.30 p.m.

5. A bus leaves the bus station at 10.48 a.m. and arrives at its destination at 2.13 p.m. How long does the journey take ?

6. How long did it take a car to travel a distance of 90 miles if it departed at 11.47 a.m., and arrived at 2.03 p.m. ?

7. How long is it from 16 minutes past ten in the morning to ten past two in the afternoon ?

8. " It is now 10.33 a.m. precisely. Meet me under the clock tower in two hours forty-nine minutes without fail !"   What time is this meeting scheduled to take place ?

9. The train leaves at 08.20. It is now 07.35. It takes 55 minutes to walk to the station. Is it possible to walk to the station in time to catch the train ?

10. It takes me twenty-five minutes to walk to the shops. It takes another one hour 45 minutes to do my shopping. Then I have to walk home again - which takes thirty-five minutes because the bags are heavy and I walk more slowly. The time now is 10.20 a.m. If I leave now, what time will I get back home ?

Timetables

The times shown on timetables are nearly always now in the twenty-four hour clock, so they should not present any great difficulty. Look at this example of an airline timetable:

LEEDS - PARIS - COLOGNE

			Flight 1		Flight 2	
Leeds	dep.		09.00		16.50	
Paris	arr.		10.15		18.40	
	dep.		11.15		19.45	
Cologne	arr.		12.05		20.40	

This timetable, which shows flights between Leeds, Paris and Cologne in Germany gives us a great deal of information. Look at the following questions, and see how they can be answered from the timetable:

(i)   How long does Flight 1 take from Leeds to Paris ?
           10.15 - 09.00 = 1 hour 15 minutes.

(ii)   How long does the plane wait at Paris airport during each flight ?
           11.15 - 10.15 = 1 hour (Flight 1); 19.45 - 18.40 = 1 hour 5 minutes (Flight 2)

(iii)   By how much is the morning flight from Leeds to Paris faster than the afternoon flight ?
           We have already worked out the time for the morning flight (Flight 1): 1 hour 15 mins.
           Afternoon flight (Flight 2): 18.40 - 16.50 = 1 hour 45 minutes.
           So the afternoon flight takes: 1 hour 45 mins.
           1 hour 45 mins. - 1 hour 15 mins. = 30 minutes longer.

(iv)   At what time on the twelve hour clock does Flight 2 leave Paris ?
           19.45 - 12 = 7.45 p.m.

(v)   What is the total journey time from Leeds to Cologne on each flight ?
           Flight 1 : 12.05 - 09.00 = 3 hours 5 mins.
           Flight 2 : 20.40 - 16.50 = 3 hours 50 mins.

(vi)   What is the actual flying time (= time in the air) on Flight 2 between Leeds and Cologne ?
           Leeds to Paris is 1 hour 45 minutes (as we have already worked out).
           Paris to Cologne is: 20.40 - 19.45 = 55 minutes.
           Add the two: 1 hour 45 mins. + 55 mins. = 2 hours 40 minutes flying time.

The following exercise is based on a timetable as well. Use the same methods to answer the questions, setting them out to show your working as has been done above.

Exercise 35 B (AT 3 Levels 4 & 5)

TIMETABLE - LONDON TO BRUSSELS

		Flight 1	Flight 2	Flight 3	Flight 4
London (Victoria Bus Station)	dep.	06.45	08.00	16.30	20.10
London (Gatwick Airport)	dep.	08.30	10.05	18.05	21.35
Brussels (International)	arr.	09.25	11.15	19.15	22.35
Brussels (Central Bus Station)	arr.	10.10	12.00	20.00	23.20

This is a timetable which shows flights between London (Gatwick) and Brussels. It also shows bus connections from the bus stations to each airport.

1.   How long does it take for a passenger to travel from bus station to bus station in the two cities on each of the four flights ?

2.   What is the actual flying time between London and Brussels by each flight ?

3.   How much time is allowed for the bus journey from Victoria to Gatwick for each flight ?

4.   How much time is allowed for the journey from Brussels airport to the bus station on each flight ?

5.   What is the difference between the shortest and longest journey time ?

TIME, DISTANCE and SPEED

We often want to know how long it will take to do something - especially to go on a journey.
We also might well want to know how fast we are travelling, and what distance we have travelled.

All these three things: time, distance and speed are linked together by mathematical equations. If we know any two of them we can always calculate the other.

It is important to learn the following three simple formulae for problems of this sort:

(1)   **Time**   = $\dfrac{\textbf{Distance}}{\textbf{Speed}}$

(2)   **Distance**   =   **Time x Speed**

(3)   **Speed**   = $\dfrac{\textbf{Distance}}{\textbf{Time}}$

Remember that when one quantity is placed over another (to form a kind of fraction), the top line must be divided by the bottom line to complete the calculation.

It is important that related units are used when using these formulae.

The normal units are: *Time is measured in hours (and fractions of an hour)*
                               Distance is measured in kilometres (and fractions of a kilometre)
                               Speed is measured in kilometres per hour (km./h. or k.p.h.)

You can of course use different measurements, so long as they are linked in the same way - with the measurement of speed combining the two units for time and distance.

Look at these three examples to show you how to do problems involving time, distance and speed:

Example (a)

A man cycles at a speed of 20 kilometres per hour. How long will it take him to cycle 40 kilometres ?

The two variables we know are speed (20 km./h.) and distance (140 km.). We have to find time.

Time   = $\dfrac{\text{Distance}}{\text{Speed}}$

Time (hours)   = $\dfrac{140 \text{ km.}}{20 \text{ km./h.}}$ =   140 km. ÷ 20 km./h.

Time   =   7 hours

Example (b)

How far will a non-stop train travelling at an average speed of 100 km./h. travel in four hours ?

The two variables we know are speed (100 km./h.) and time (4 hours). We have to find distance.

Distance   =   Time x Speed

Distance (km.) =   4 hours x 100 km./h.

Distance   =   400 km.

Example (c)

A motorway coach covers 175 kilometres in 2.5 hours. What is its average speed ?

The two variables we know are distance (175 km.) and time (2.5 hours). We have to find speed.

Speed   = $\dfrac{\text{Distance}}{\text{Time}}$

Speed (k.p.h.) = $\dfrac{175 \text{ km.}}{2.5 \text{ h.}}$ =   175 km. ÷ 2.5 h.

Speed   =   70 k.p.h.

You may sometimes need to change the units in which a problem is set for convenience of working (and then change them back again for the answer), or you may be asked to give your answer in different units.

If you are changing **to a bigger unit of TIME** (seconds to minutes etc.) you will need to **multiply** by the number of smaller units in the bigger unit.
If you are changing **to a smaller unit of TIME**, you will need to **divide** by that figure.

If you are changing **to a bigger unit of DISTANCE** (kilometres to metres etc.) you will need to **divide** by the number of smaller units in the bigger unit.
If you are changing **to a smaller unit of DISTANCE**, you will need to **multiply** by that figure.

Look at this example for the method:

Example (d)

A fast train travels at the speed of two kilometres per minute.
(a)   What is its speed in km./h. ? (b)   What is its speed in metres per minute ?

(a)   An hour is a unit of TIME.
         An hour is a larger unit than a minute.
         There are 60 minutes in an hour.
         So we must multiply by 60:
         2 km./min. x 60 = 120 km./h.

78

(b)   An metre is a unit of DISTANCE.
       A metre is a smaller unit than a kilometre.
       There are 1 000 metres in a kilometre.
       So we must multiply by 1 000:
       2 km./min. x 1 000 = 2 000 metres per minute.

Exercise 36

1.   A plane flies at an average speed of 480 km./h. How far will it travel in four hours ?

2.   How far can a person cycle in six hours at an average speed of 33 km./h. ?

3.   A plane flies 6 300 kilometres in twelve hours. What is its average speed ?

      (a)   In kilometres per hour   (b)   In kilometres per minute

4.   To keep to its timetable, a train has to travel 360 kilometres in four hours. What average
      speed must it maintain to be on time ?

5.   The distance between two towns is 750 kilometres. How long will it take a car travelling
      at an average speed of fifty km./h. to get from one town to the other ?

Exercise 36 A   Problems

1.   Express the following speeds in metres per second:
      (a)   72 km./h.   (b)   12 km./h.   (c)   180 km./h.

2.   Express the following speeds in kilometres per hour:
      (a)   100 m./sec.   (b)   15 km. in a quarter of an hour   (c)   300 metres a minute

3.   The non-stop coach leaves at 09.25, and arrives at its destination at 12.25. The stopping bus
      takes the same route, but arrives exactly one hour later. The total route distance is 180 km.
      How much faster, on average, does the non-stop coach travel than the stopping bus ?

4.   The 08.15 train from Derby to London travels at an average of 90 km./h. to cover the
      120 miles of the journey. What time does it arrive ?

5.   Two groups of children set off set off from Splodge Street School at the same time.
      Group One is going to visit Spooky Hollow House. Group Two is going to visit Gruesomeville
      Museum. Group One sets off at 09.00, and Group Two sets off at 09.30.
      Group One travelled at an average speed of 12 km./h. and arrived at 12.00 hours.
      Group Two travelled arrived at 11.00 hours after a journey of 27 km.

      (a)   Which is further from the school, Spooky Hollow House, or Gruesomeville Museum,
             and by what distance ?

      (b)   Which group travelled faster, and by what speed ?

PERCENTAGES

When we want to compare two or more fractions, it is often convenient to consider both or all of them with a denominator of one hundred. This tells us how many parts out of a hundred are being considered in each case. Fractions with a denominator of 100 are called *Percentages*.

Instead of writing the percentage as a fraction over 100, there is a special sign for it: **%** .

The percentage sign is just another way of writing a fraction - often one of several ways:

$1/2$ = $50/100$ = 0.5 = 50 % (fifty percent).

$1/4$ = $25/100$ = 0.25 = 25 % (twenty-five percent).

In solving problems, you can use any of the equivalent forms shown in the two examples above. Try to select the one which will involve the least complicated figures (unless you are instructed to use one particular form).

Converting a Decimal Fraction into a Percentage

You will have noticed in the examples above, how similar decimals are to percentages. They already use the same figures. The simple thing to remember is that any digit in the *tenths* column in a decimal fraction belongs in the *tens* column in the equivalent percentage. Any digit in the *hundredths* column in a decimal belongs in the *units* column in a percentage.

There is a short way to work it out if it is not immediately obvious:
Move the decimal two places to the left across the decimal point (i.e. Multiply it by 100).
The result is the percentage figure. (Do not forget to insert the % sign.)

Example (a)

Change 0.375 into a percentage.

Move the decimal two places to the right across the point, which gives us 37.5   Add the % sign: 37.5 %
It is as simple as that.

Converting a Percentage into a Decimal Fraction

To do this you have to reverse the process. Divide the percentage by 100, and insert a decimal point.

Example (b)

Change 30 % into a decimal fraction.

To divide 30 by 100, we can insert a decimal point (30.00), and then move the digits two places to the left across the decimal point. So we now have 0.30. Which we can simply write as 0.3.

Converting a Vulgar Fraction into a Percentage

You have seen that the short way to convert a decimal into a percentage is to multiply by 100. This is also the way to convert a vulgar fraction. Since 100 written in the form of a fraction is $^{100}/_1$ you are in fact only multiplying the top line (numerator).

Do not forget to cancel if possible.

Example (c)

Change $^3/_5$ *into a percentage.*

$$^3/_5 \text{ x } ^{100}/_1$$

You can cancel the denominator 5 and the numerator 100 by 5 to make the multiplication easier.

$$^3/_{\cancel{5}\,1} \text{ x } ^{20}\cancel{100}/_1 = ^{60}/_1 . \; (^{60}/_1 \text{ is the same as 60.)}$$

So the answer is 60 % .

Converting a Percentage into a Vulgar Fraction

To do this you have to reverse the process.

Divide the percentage by 100 ($^{100}/_1$).

Remember that in dividing by fractions you have to turn the divisor upside down and multiply.

(So in fact you will be multiplying by: $^1/_{100}$.)

In fact there is a very simple way to do this.
Just write the percentage as a vulgar fraction with a denominator of 100.

Then all you need to do is cancel the fraction if possible.

Example (d)

Change 55 % into a vulgar fraction.

First write the percentage as a vulgar fraction over 100: $^{55}/_{100}$.
(This is the equivalent of dividing by 100.)

Then all you have to do is cancel.
In this case the numerator and denominator can both be divided by five:

$$^{\cancel{55}\,11}/_{\cancel{100}\,20}$$

So: 55 % = $^{11}/_{20}$

Exercise 37

(1)   Change the following decimals into percentages:

    (a)   0.27   (b)   0.273   (c)   0.537   (d)   0.623   (e)   0.039

(2)   Change the following vulgar fractions into percentages:

    (a) $^4/_5$ (b) $^7/_{10}$ (c) $^{13}/_{20}$ (d) $^{17}/_{25}$ (e) $^{19}/_{50}$

(3)   Change the following percentages into decimals:

    (a)   3 %   (b)   90 %   (c)   27.5 %   (d)   10 %   (e)   0.5 %

(4)   Change the following percentages into vulgar fractions:

    (a)   24 %   (b)   8 %   (c)   76 %   (d)   120 %   (e)   0.5 %

FINDING THE PERCENTAGE

The most common use of percentages is in statements about a particular percentage of an amount or quantity. You may very often have to work out this sort of percentage problem.

The method is not difficult:

(i)   Turn the percentage into a vulgar fraction
(ii)   Cancel into its lowest form to simplify the calculation
(iii)   Multiply the figure or amount by the fraction (because *of* means *multiply*).

Example (e)

Find 10 % of 60.

First change the percentage into a fraction: $10 \% = {}^1/_{10}$

It will not cancel, so we then multiply: $^1/_{10}$ x $^{60}/_1$

We can cancel in this multiplication, dividing both ten and sixty by 10:

$^1/_{\cancel{10}\,1}$ x $^{6}\cancel{60}/_1 = {}^6/_1 = 6.$

Example (f)

What is 25 % of £150

Change the percentage into a fraction: $25 \% = {}^{25}/_{100}$

This fraction can be cancelled (by dividing by 25): $^{1}\cancel{25}/_{\cancel{100}\,4}$

Multiply: $^1/_4$ x £ $^{150}/_1$.

Cancel again (by dividing by 2): $^1/_{4\,2}$ x £ $^{75}\cancel{150}/_1$

$^1/_2$ x £ $^{75}/_1 = £ {}^{75}/_2 = £ 37.50.$

Another kind of question you may be asked is one where you know what a particular percentage of a certain figure is, and you have to find the figure itself.

The way to do this is by finding *one* percent first. You do this by dividing by the number of percent. Then you find 100 % by multiplying your result by 100.

Example (g)

44 % of the length of a piece of cloth is 110 cm. How long is the entire piece of cloth ?

44 %   = 110 cm.

So 1 %   = $^{110}/_{44}$ cm.

Simplify this fraction by cancelling by 11: $^{10}{}^{\cancel{110}}/_{\cancel{44}\,4}$, and again by 2: $^{5}{}^{\cancel{10}}/_{\cancel{4}\,2}$. Result: $^{5}/_{2}$.

Now you know one percent of the total, all you have to do is multiply by 100 to find 100 %.

$^{5}/_{2}$ x $^{100}/_{1}$ = $^{500}/_{2}$. Simplify by cancelling: $^{250}{}^{\cancel{500}}/_{\cancel{2}\,1}$ = 250.

So the total length is 250 cm.

Exercise 38

(1)   Find the following percentages:
         (a)   75 % of £ 3.60   (b)   80 % of £ 5.50   (c)   120% of 1 000 litres
         (d)   27 % of 200 metric tons.   (e)   90 % of 4.50 km. (Answer in metres.)

(2)   There are 25 children in a class. One day twenty percent were absent with 'flu.
         (a)   How many children were absent ?   (b)   How many children were present ?

(3)   A cinema has 680 seats. At one performance 85 % of the seats were occupied. How many seats were occupied ?

(4)   124 000 pupils sat an examination. 24 % of them failed. How many pupils passed ?

(5)   45 % of the pupils in a school are girls. There are 220 boys in the school.
         (a)   How many girls are in the school ?   (b)   How many pupils are there altogether ?

(6)   Last year there were 105 road accidents in Anville District. This year the number decreased by 40 %. How many accidents were there this year ?

(7)   Ripple and Offset Ltd., Estate Agents, received a 7 $^{1}/_{2}$ % commission on the sale price of a plot of land sold for £ 18 720. How much money did they receive ?

(8)   A retailer paid a wholesaler £ 2.50 per item for a batch of 250 shirts. He then increased the price of each shirt by 15 % for sale in his shop. In a week he had sold all 250.
         (a)   How much money did he take for all the shirts ?
         (b)   How much profit did he make ? (Profit is selling price minus buying price.)

AVERAGES

The word **average** means something like **middle point**. It is often convenient to find out what is the mid-point or average of a whole group of numbers or measurements.
Another word often used in mathematics for average is **mean**.

There is a simple formula for working out averages:

Average   =   <u>Sum of the quantities</u>
Number of quantities

The sum of the quantities means the result of adding together all the different numbers or measurements or amounts that you have.

The number of quantities is the number of different figures you have.

You find the average by dividing the first by the second.

Example (a)

Find the average of these sums of money: £ 2.50 ;   £ 1.20 ;   £ 2.10 ;   £ 2.20 .

First add them up to find the "sum of the quantities": £ 2.50 + £ 1.20 + £ 2.10 + £ 2.20 = £ 8.00 .

Now you have to divide this by the "number of quantities", and there are just four amounts.

So: £ 8.00 ÷ 4   =   £ 2.00 , and that is the average of these four sums of money.

Sometimes you may get a question where you know the average and are asked to find the total.
In this case you multiply the average by the number of the quantities.

Example (b)

I spent an average of £ 6.30 per day when I was on holiday. My holiday lasted seven days.
How much did I spend ?

The average is £ 6.30. The number of quantities is seven (seven days).

So the total spent is: £ 6.30 x 7 = £ 44.10 .

It is also possible to work out the number of quantities if you know the sum of quantities and the average. Simply divide the sum of the quantities by the average.

Exercise 39

(1) Find the average of these amounts: £ 2.00 ; £ 2.60 ; £ 2.90 .

(2) Find the average of these numbers: 184 ; 72 ; 58 ; 82 ; 64 .

(3) Find the average of these weights: 240 g. ; 480 g. ; 420 g.

(4) Find the average of these amounts: £ 250 ; £ 120 ; £ 210 ; £ 210 .

(5) Find the average of these lengths: 1.04 m. ; 56 cm. ; 200 mm. ; 580 mm. **

** *Notice that it is necessary to work with all quantities in the same units. If you get a question like this one, decide which unit is most convenient and convert the other quantities to it. (In this case it is cm.)*

Exercise 39 A   Problems (for Levels 4 and 5)

(1) In a family the ages of the children are:
Bill 7 years; John 12 years; Sarah 3 years; the twins (Andrew and Anne) 14 years.
(a)   What is the average age of the children ?
(b)   What is the average age of the boys ?
(c)   What is the average age of the girls ?

(2) During a two week holiday, I walked an average of 9 km. a day.
How far did I walk altogether ?

(3) The children in a whole class scored a grand total of 5 481 marks in their exams.
The average mark for the class was 203. How many children are there in the class ?

(4) Here is a table of results for six children in three exams (each of them marked out of 50):

	English	Maths	Science
Ahmed	45	37	45
John	29	24	37
Elizabeth	43	32	49
Usha	28	20	30
Nithya	46	48	50
Ryan	25	22	26

Work out the following:
(a)   The average mark for each subject
(b)   The average mark for each child.
(c)   The overall average (all children, all subjects).

(5) The average of three numbers is 57.
The average of the first two of these numbers is 49.
What is the third number ?
(Clue: This is a trick question. It is a lot easier than it seems.)

RATIO

A ratio is a comparison between two similar quantities.

For example, in a class, the ratio of boys to girls might be three *to* two.
Ratios are usually written with a colon (**:**) between the two groups or quantities. This is always read as the word **to**. So: boys : girls (boys to girls); 3 : 2 (three to two).

Ratios can always be written as fractions. The numerators (top lines) will be the two figures for the ratio; the denominator (bottom line) will be the sum of the two figures for the ratios.

So in the example above we could just as easily write: $^3/_5$ of the class are boys, and $^2/_5$ are girls.

Notice that ratios can be written with either figure first, so long as it is made clear which quantity is which when you are talking about something other than simple numbers.
Also notice that ratios can contain three or more quantities as well as just two. For example: 3 : 4 : 5.

It is of course important that the units for both parts of a ratio (or for both parts of a fraction) are the same. If they are different, choose which unit is easiest to work with and convert. Always show a ratio in its simplest possible form.

Example (a)

Show the ratio 15 cm. to 4 metres in its simplest form.

The first step is to convert into the same units: 4 m. = 400 cm.

So now the ratio can be written: 15 : 400

The next step is to write the ratio as a fraction: $^{15}/_{400}$

The fraction can then be cancelled (by five): $^{3}\cancel{15}/\cancel{400}\,_{80}$

We can then rewrite it as a ratio: 80 : 3 or 3 : 80 .

Exercise 40

Write the following as ratios in their lowest terms:

1.   7 p. to £3.00   2.   5 mm. to 1 cm.   3.   40 g. to 200 g.

4.   370 g. to 2 kg.   5.   48 cm. to 3 m.   6.   160 p. to £4.80

7.   750 ml. to 2 litres   8. $3\,^1/_2$ to 14   9.   180 to 729

10. $^7/_8$ to $^3/_4$.

FINDING THE VALUE OF RATIOS

The formula for finding the value of the parts in a ratio is quite simple:

(i)   Add the two (or more) figures in the ratio together.
This gives you the total number of shares.

(ii)   Divide the total amount by the number of shares.
This gives you the value of one share.

(iii)   Multiply each figure in the ratio by the value of one share.
This gives you the value of each figure in the ratio.

Look at these two examples to show how it is done:

Example (b)

Share £ 20.00 in the ratio of 2 : 3 .

(i)   To find the number of shares we add the figures in the ratio: $2 + 3 = 5$.

(ii)   To find the value of one share divide the total by the number of shares: $£ 20 \div 5 = £ 4$.

(iii)   Multiply both figures in the ratio by the value of one share: $2 \times £ 4 = £ 8$
$3 \times £ 4 = £ 12$

Notice that the two figures in your answer could still be written as a ratio: $8 : 12$, but this would no longer be in its simplest form.

Also notice that you can check your result by adding the two figures. The result should be the total figure you are working with: $£ 8 + £ 12 = £ 20$. So the result is correct.

Example (c)

Divide a four metre length of cloth in the ratio: one to three to four.

(i)   To find the number of shares we add the figures in the ratio: $1 + 3 + 4 = 8$.

(ii)   To find the value of one share divide the total by the number of shares: 4 m. $\div$ 8 .
In this case it is convenient to convert the metres into centimetres: 400 cm. $\div$ 8 = 50 cm.

(iii)   Multiply each figure in the ratio by the value of one share: 1×50 cm. $= 50$ cm.
3×50 cm. $= 150$ cm.
4×50 cm. $= 200$ cm.

(You could then convert 150 cm. and 200 cm. back to 1 m. 50 cm. and 2 m. respectively.)

It is very difficult to go wrong, so long as you go through the steps carefully and show your working.

Pro Rata Changing

You can also use ratios to work out changes in one item in a combination. If you have several items in ratio to each other, and you increase or decrease one, you have to increase or decrease the others in the same proportion. *Pro rata* is an expression which means *in proportion*.

The rule is simple. If you multiply or divide one item in a ratio by a given figure, you must multiply or divide the other items in the ratio by the same figure.

This example will show you how it works:

Example (d)

To make a cake I need to use 200 g. of butter and 160 g. of caster sugar. By mistake I put in 400 g. of butter. How much caster sugar will I now need ?

The amount of butter in the cake should be 200 g. In fact it is 400 g.
This is twice as much - so we have multiplied the amount of butter by two.
That means we must do the same to the amount of caster sugar: 160 g. x 2 = 320 g.

Similarly, if we want to increase all the quantities in a given ratio, we can do it, so long as we increase them all pro rata: in the same proportion.

Example (e)

To make a cake for four people I need to use 200 g. of butter and 160 g. of caster sugar.
How much will I need of each to make a cake for 12 people?

How much bigger is the cake ? It was for 4 people; now it is for 12.
So it is 3 times bigger (3 x 4 = 12).
So all the quantities involved must also be three times greater: 200 g x 3 = 600 g. of butter
160 g x 3 = 480 g. of caster sugar.

Exercise 41

1. In a class of 33 pupils, the boy : girl ratio is 6 : 5 .
   How many boys and how many girls are there in the class ?

2. Divide a piece of cloth 12 m. long in the ratio 6 : 4 : 2.

3. Peter, Sandra and Louise share a total weekly pocket money allowance of £ 5.00 in the ratio of their ages. Peter is 9, Sandra is 8 and Louise is 3. How much does each child get ?

4. A town's population is 69 124. The ratio of males to females is 6 : 5. How many males and how many females are there in the town ?

5. To make a cake to serve eight people you need: 400 g. of butter, 320 g. of caster sugar, 2 eggs, and 800 g. of self-raising flour.
   (a) If 600 g. of butter is used, what amounts of the other ingredients are required ?
   (b) What quantities of each ingredient are needed to make a cake to serve four people ?

PROPORTION

You have already seen something of how proportion works when adjusting ratios pro rata.

Generally in problems involving proportion, you are told the total for a given number of units, and then told to calculate the total for a different number of units.

The simple key to proportion problems is this:
> *Always start by calculating the value of one unit.*

The following examples show you how this works:

Example (a)

If six metres of cloth cost £ 7.80, how much will nine metres cost ?

The unit we are looking for here is metres.
You know that six metres cost £ 7.80. How much will *one* metre cost ?
That is simple: £ 7.80 ÷ 6 = £ 1.30 .
To find nine metres you simply need to multiply by 9:   £ 1.30 x 9 = £ 11.70

If you are not sure whether to multiply or divide, just think whether you are looking for a smaller amount, in which case you divide, or a larger amount, in which case you multiply.

Problems involving time are more tricky, because it is very easy to multiply when you should divide. Look at the following example, which has two stages in the problem posed:

Example (b)

Two workmen dig a hole in three days. How long will it take six workmen to dig a whole twice the size if they work at exactly the same rate.

The unit we are looking for here is days. (We have to find how long something will take.)
We know that two workmen take three days. How long will one workman take ?

This is the trick part of the question. One workman will take twice the time (not half the time).
So one workman takes: 2 x 3 = 6 days.

How long will six workmen take ? Another trick ! Six workman will not take six times as long, they will only take one sixth of the time, so you must divide by 6, not multiply: 6 ÷ 6 = 1 .

Do not forget the second part of the question. You know how long it would take six workmen to dig the original hole. But you are asked how long they will take to dig a hole twice as big. There is no trick involved this time: it is twice as big, so it will take twice as long: 1 x 2 = 2 days.

In this sort of problem involving time taken it is important to use your common sense. It is obvious that (other things being equal) one person will take twice as long as two people to do the same thing.

If you are looking at an obviously shorter time, divide.

If you are looking at an obviously longer time, multiply.

Exercise 42

1. If two oil-drums between them hold 280 litres of oil, how many litres would twelve drums of exactly the same size hold ?

2. If five pencils cost 90 p. , what will sixteen pencils cost ?

3. The total price of 23 packets of sweets is £ 6.90 . How much will eleven packets cost ?

4. A contract receptionist earns £ 135.00 for six hours' work.
    How much does she earn in 24 hours ?

5. Twelve metres of light-weight wire weigh 360 g. What will be the weight of five metres of medium weight wire, which weighs exactly twice as much per metre as light-weight wire ?

6. Twelve cameras cost £ 1 860 in total. In a month a shop sells four of the cameras.
    How much money does the shop take for the cameras it has sold ?

7. One man takes 2 hours to mow the lawn. How long will it take two boys to do the job if they only work half as fast as the man ?

8. Twenty men can pave a yard in twelve days. How long would it take 15 men at the same speed ?

Exercise 42 A   Harder Problems

1. If three men can do the work of five boys, how long will it take ten boys to dig a ditch which three men can dig in nine days ?

2. It takes six lorries a total of three complete days and twelve hours altogether to remove a load of rubbish. How many lorries of the same type would you need to get the job done in twelve hours ?

3. Six girls work a paper-round covering forty-nine houses each. They all get paid the same amount, and in a week they earn £ 49.74 between them. The newsagent decides to take on five more paper rounds, and employs another five girls at the same rate. What is his new wages bill for all his newspaper-girls ?

4. A plumber, who earns £ 40.00 per hour, takes 1 hour 30 minutes to mend three burst pipes in the council drainage depot.
    (a)   How many similar burst pipes will he have to mend to earn £ 180.00 ?
    (b)   How many hours work will this involve ?
    (c)   If his mate works half as fast for half the pay, how many hours must he work to earn £ 180, and how many pipes will he mend in that time ?

UNEQUAL SHARING

Unequal sharing occurs when something must be divided into two parts which are not equal.

In problems connected with equal sharing you will generally know the difference between the two shares, and the total to be shared.

The steps for solving unequal sharing problems are as follows:

(i)   Subtract the difference between the two shares from the total amount.

(ii)   Divide the result by 2.
        This gives the smaller share.

(iii)   Add the difference between shares to the smaller share.
        This gives the larger share.

Check your answer by adding together the two shares. The result should be the original total.

Example (a)

In a school class there are four more boys than girls. There are 36 children in the class.
How many boys are in the class ?

(i)   Subtract the difference between the two 'shares' (4) from the total (36): $36 - 4 = 32$.

(ii)   Divide the result by 2 to get the smaller 'share' (the number of girls): $32 \div 2 = 16$.

(ii)   Add the difference (4) to the smaller 'share' to get the larger (number of boys): $16 + 4 = 20$.

So there are twenty boys in the class.

Exercise 43

1.   In a school of 400 children there are 50 more girls than boys. How many boys are there ?

2.   There are five more girls than boys in a class of 31 children. How many girls are there ?

3.   David and Rachel have £ 1.70 between them. If Rachel has 20 p. more than David, how much money does David have ?

4.   Two girls pool their money to buy a toy. Salima puts 37 p. more than Janice into the total, which comes to £ 3.49 . How much does each girl put in ?

5.   A piece of cloth of area 17 square metres must be divided into two sections such that one section is three square metres larger than the other. What is the area of each section ?

UNEQUAL SHARING BETWEEN THREE

Unequal sharing when something must be divided into *three* parts which are not equal is much harder. In this sort of problem you are generally told the total, together with two of the combinations of shares, and asked to work out each separate share.

The method used is different:

(i)   Give each of the shares a letter. So you can call the three shares: A, B, and C.
       (This is just to make it simpler in referring to each share.)
       You will be told the total, together with the value of A + B, and B + C.

(ii)   Subtract (A + B) from the total.
       This gives you the value of share C.

(iii) Subtract the value of C (which you now know) from (B + C).
       This gives you the value of share B.

(iv)   Subtract the value of B (which you now know) from (A + B).
       This gives you the value of A.

Check your result by adding up the three shares, which should come to the original total.

Example (b)

In a competition, David and Ian scored 102 points between them, while David and Brendan scored 88 points between them. If the total score was 150, how many points did each boy score ?

(i)   Give each boy a letter - in this case their initials: D, I, and B.
       Write down the information you have: D + I = 102
                                                 D + B = 88
                                                 Total   = 150.

(ii)   Subtract (D + I) from the total: 150 - 102 = 48.
       So the score for B is 48.

(iii) Subtract the value of B (which you now know) from (D + B):   88 - 48 = 40
       So the score for D is 40.

(iv)   Subtract the value of D (which you now know) from (D + I):   102 - 40 = 62
       So the score for I is 62.

Scores: David: 40
              Ian: 62
              Brendan: 48

Check your result by adding the three scores together: 48 + 40 + 62 = 150.

Exercise 44

1. Three cricketers make 129 runs between them. Stonewall and Sloggett had a partnership of 106 runs. Then Stonewall and Scamper had a partnership of 68. How many runs did each batsman score ?

2. A piece of steel tubing, measuring 16 metres is to be divided into three unequal sections, such that the two end sections together measure 12 metres, and one end section plus the middle section measures 14 metres. What are the lengths of the three sections ?

3. In an archery competition, R.Hood and W.Scarlett between them scored 305 points, while R.Hood and F.Tuck scored 200 points between them. The total score for all three competitors was 409 points. What did each competitor score ?

4. Two children and their mother share a one litre bottle of lemonade.
   Jack and Mrs. Hill together drink 700 ml. Jill and Mrs. Hill together drink 500 ml.
   How much does each of them drink ?

5. Three football teams in the league competition score the following number of goals:

Arsenal and Blackburn together:	43
Arsenal and Aston Villa together:	41
The three teams together:	56

   How many does each team score ?

GRAPHS

Graphs are a way of showing number facts in picture form.
The simplest form of graph is the tally chart. Tally charts are used when you are counting things.
Here is an example of one used for a traffic survey:

VEHICLE	TALLY	No.
Cars	卌 卌 卌 卌 IIII	24
Buses	II	2
Lorries	卌 II	7
Vans	卌 卌 II	12
Mo/bikes	卌	5
Bikes	卌 I	6
	TOTAL	56

Traffic on Woody Lane: 10.00 - 11.00

The way tallying works is that an upright line or mark is made for each item (in this case each vehicle), but the fifth one is shown as a diagonal line across the first four. So you have the numbers arranged in groups of five. (Most people can count in fives very easily, so this is a convenient way of displaying information, and also makes it easy to add up the final total.)

A tally chart is very nearly a graph already, and it can easily be converted into one.
Here is a bar graph which shows the same information:

TRAFFIC SURVEY ON WOODY LANE - 10.00 to 11.00 hours.

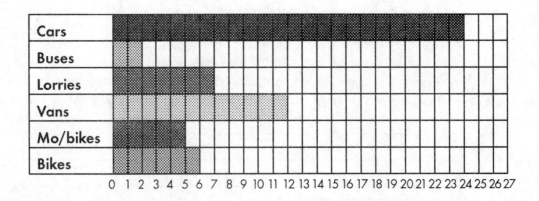

You can see immediately by looking at the graph how the different totals compare.

Bar graphs can be drawn like this, as horizontal bar graphs, or they can be drawn with the 'bars' going up and down - as vertical bar graphs. On the next page the same graph is shown as a vertical bar graph. Vertical bar graphs are more common

A vertical bar graph which shows the same information:

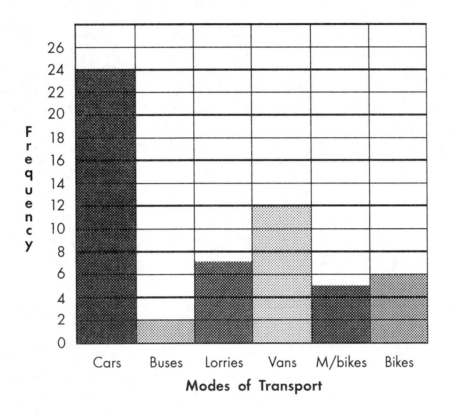

There are two interesting things to notice about this bar graph:

Firstly, not all the numbers in the scale at the side are shown. The lines going across are not drawn at: 1, 2, 3, 4, 5 etc. Instead they are drawn at 2, 4, 6, 8, 10 etc. You can use any scale you like in drawing a graph, so long as the intervals are all the same.

Secondly, you can see how to deal with a number that comes between two levels on a scale. This graph shows four and six, but does not show five. So we have to estimate the half-way mark between four and six and draw a line across to represent five, and similarly with seven. Even on graphs where every number is shown this can still happen, as you may have to estimate a half or a quarter.

Sometimes bar graphs are drawn in such a way that the bars only appear as lines. This kind of graph is sometimes called a 'line graph', but that is rather confusing since this name is also used for a different kind of graph. Here is an example of this sort of line/bar graph (again showing the same information):

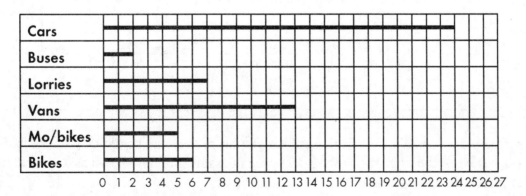

95

You have already seen one sort of line graph. The other, much more common sort, to which the term usually applies shows a continuous line (usually a sloping one), which plots linked information.

For this sort of graph there are two *axes*. Learnt this word *axes*. It is pronounced *ax -ees*, and is the plural of *axis*. The vertical axis shows one measurement, and the horizontal axis shows another.

So for example, if we want to plot on a graph how long something takes, we would have one axis showing time and another showing distance. You might also have a line graph plotting average ages against average heights. Or you could do one plotting average height against average weight. These are both possible graphs to draw up for a school. If your teacher will let you do this as an activity, you should start by drawing up a tally chart, and then turning it into a line graph.

Example (a)

Suppose you are on an aeroplane, and you check the distance flown at various times into the flight. (This is conveniently shown on the video screen at regular intervals.) At one hour, it is 400 km. At two hours it is 800 km. At three hours, you are having your dinner, so you forget to check. At four hours it is 1 600 km. At five hours it is 2 000 km. At six and seven hours you are asleep, so you do not check. At eight hours you check for the last time, and the distance is 3 200 km. At exactly 8 hours 30 minutes the plane lands.

All this sounds very complicated, but it can be put on a graph very easily. Here is the graph it makes. Study it carefully, and then turn to the next page to see how it is derived.

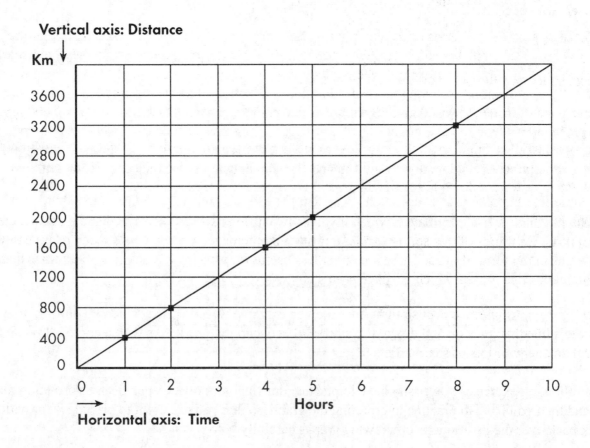

First draw the two axes, one down the left hand side, and one along the bottom. Label the vertical axis distance, and drawn horizontal lines across from it at regular intervals. In this case we will use 400 km. as the interval between the lines. Makes sure all the lines are the same distance apart. Next label the horizontal axis along the bottom as Time, and divide it up into similar intervals, with vertical lines. For this axis the interval most convenient is one hour.

Now you can plot your information on the graph. Start with the first time, one hour, and go up the line till it crosses the horizontal line for the first distance, 400 kilometres. There make a clear mark - a dot or a cross. Then go to the next time. Follow up the line till it crosses the horizontal line for the next distance, 800 km. Make another mark. Go on to the next time, four hours (not three), and go up till you cross the 1 600 km horizontal line. Make another mark. Continue in the same way till you have a mark for each observation. Then join up the marks. The result is the completed line graph.

Look back at the graph, and check off each stage of the drawing process with the instructions above. It is quite a useful exercise to draw the graph yourself, following the instructions.

One very useful thing about this sort of graph is that it can be drawn with only limited information. Though there was not a record for the distance at each hour in this case, it was still possible to complete the graph.

The most interesting thing, however, is that it is possible to use the graph to fill in the missing information. We can see straight away what the distance was at three hours - because the line of the graph intersects (= crosses) the three hour line at exactly the point it crosses the 1 200 km. line. In the same way we can say that the plane has flown 2 400 km. at exactly six hours, because that is the point where the line of the graph indicates the intersection.

We can also work out fractions of the hours from this graph. Suppose we want to know how far the plane has got in seven and a half hours. We estimate half way between the seven and eight hour marks, and take a line straight up to the point where it intersects with the line of the graph. From that point we take a horizontal straight line along to the distance axis on the left. It meets the axis exactly half way between the 2 800 and the 3 200 km. marks, so we can easily work out that the distance is 3 000 km.

In the same way, we might want to know how long the plane would take to fly 3 600 km. We simply follow the line from 3 600 km. across till it intersects with the line of the graph. From that point we follow the line straight down to the time axis, and get the answer of nine hours.

You can of course show information which involves two different items (like speed and distance: the correct name for things of this sort is *variables*) with a bar graph, or a graph where the bars are shown as columns in the form of lines. These are rather less useful for working out unknown quantities than the continuous line graphs which we have been studying.

Not all line graphs produce neat straight lines like the example we have used. When the information produces a line that goes up and down, it is normal practice to join the marks with a curved flowing line, rather than one with lots of sharp points in it.

In the following exercises you firstly have to practice drawing your own graphs from information given to you, and then you have to practice interpreting the graph, so that you can use it to provide information. Check back over the instructions on drawing graphs carefully before you start.

Exercise 45

1. Here is a tally chart showing the favourite colours of the 54 children in year six at St. Alphege's School:

COLOUR	TALLY	No.
Red	||||| ||||| ||||| ||	
Green	||||| ||||	
Blue	||||| ||||| |||||		
Orange	|||	
Purple	||||	
Yellow	|||||	
		TOTAL	

Favourite colours

(a) Copy the tally chart, and fill in the totals.

(b) Draw a vertical bar chart to show the information.
(Think carefully about what scale to use for your bar chart.)

(c) Write a table of the colours in order of popularity, with the most popular first.

2. A boy was asked to do a survey of the heights of all the children in his school year. He did not know how to draw up a tally chart or how to make a graph. So this is what he did:

128 cm.	/	130 cm.	/////	131 cm.	////////
132 cm.	//////////	133 cm.	//////////////	134 cm.	///////
135 cm.	/////////	136 cm.	///	138 cm.	//
140 cm.	/				

(a) Write the information properly in the form of a tally chart. (Remember to include the heights in the series - which he left blank - as zero entries.)

(b) Draw a bar graph to show the information.

(c) Draw a vertical chart using an upright line instead of a bar for each height. (This is the first sort of "line graph" we mentioned - not the sort with points on a line.)

3. A group of girls go for a hike in the country. After two hours they have covered eight kilometres. After three hours the total distance is twelve kilometres. In the next hour and a half they cover another six kilometres. At the end of the day, after six hours' walking they have made a journey of 24 kilometres.

Plot a continuous line graph from the information you are given here. Draw the two axes using convenient measurements and intervals. Clearly show the points you have marked on, and join them up with one continuous straight line.

Exercise 45 A

1. In the window of a local butcher's shop there are four freezer packs of meat.
    The first is labelled: 1 kg.   £ 7.00
    The second is labelled: 2 kg.   £ 14.00
    The third is labelled: 2.5 kg. £ 17.50
    The fourth is labelled: 3.5 kg. £ 24.50

    (a)   Draw a continuous line graph to show this information. (Think carefully about the
          scale you use for the half kg. and 50 p. values. It is important in this question.)

    (b)   Using the line graph, work out the following:
          (i)   How much would a half-kilogram pack of meat cost ?
          (ii)   How much would a five kilogram pack cost ?
          (iii)   What size pack could be bought for £ 21.00 ?
          (iv)   What size pack could be bought for £ 10.50 ?
          (v)   What is the price of meat per kilogram ?

2. Here is a line graph which shows the distance travelled by a non-stop train and the time it
    takes for the journey.

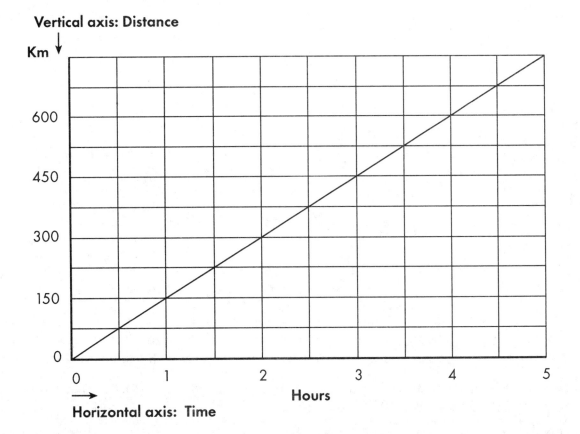

    (a)   How far has the train travelled after three hours ?
    (b)   How far has it travelled after four and a half hours ?
    (c)   How long does it take to travel 600 kilometres ?
    (d)   How long does it take to travel 375 kilometres ?
    (e)   What is its speed in kph. ?

PIE CHARTS

A pie chart is given this name because it is round and can be cut into pieces - like a pie !

It is a simple and effective way of showing information. Each segment or portion of the pie shows by its size how much there is of a particular item. It is important when drawing a pie chart to get the segments in the correct proportion to each other.

Here are three pie charts, which show how the three children in a family spent the same two hour period one evening. The time for each child is divided up into different activities, and the pie charts do show very clearly just how much time each child spends on each.

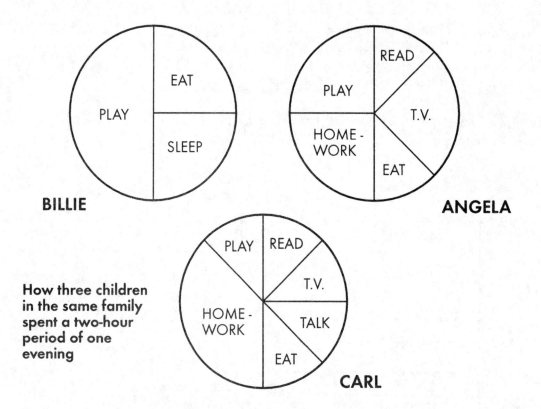

BILLIE

ANGELA

How three children in the same family spent a two-hour period of one evening

CARL

So we can see at once that Billie spends half of his two hours (which is one hour) playing. The remaining hour is divided into two half-hour periods of eating and sleeping.

Angela only spends a quarter of the time playing (which works out at half an hour). She spends the same amount of time doing homework, and the same again watching television. The remaining half hour is divided into two - a quarter of an hour eating, and another quarter of an hour reading.

Carl spends five periods of a quarter of an hour each on playing, reading, television, eating and talking. He spends three quarters of an hour doing his homework.

You should have been able to work out that each of the small segments of the pie stand for an eighth of the time, and since the time is two hours, one eight of it is a quarter of an hour.

Notice how much information we can get from this pie chart.
(If you were told that one of the children is thirteen, one is eleven, and one is three years old, could you make an intelligent guess, from the information on the pie chart, which was which ?)

Exercise 46

1. The children in a class were asked what their favourite drink was.
    Five eighths of them said lemonade.
    One quarter of them said milk shakes.
    One eighth of them said orange squash.

Draw a pie chart which shows the above results. *(Try to get the divisions (eighths) all roughly the same size. It may help you to divide the pie into eight pieces first, and then mark off the real divisions by colouring them.)* **

2. In a class of 30 children a count was done of the different hair colour. These are the results:
    Red or auburn hair: 3
    Yellow or blond hair: 6
    Brown hair: 12
    Black hair: 9

Draw a pie chart to show the above results. *(You need to start by dividing your pie into ten equal segments. All the above figures are an exact number of tenths.)* **

3. Here is a pie chart which shows four hours of a school day, and how they are used:

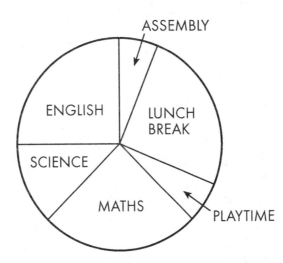

With this chart, the basic division is into eighths. But only one of the segments of the pie is actually one eighth. That is the part labelled science. You also have two very small divisions - each of which is half of the basic one eighth division.

(a) How long is spent on each school subject ?
(b) How long altogether is spent on lessons ?
(c) How long is spent altogether on other things ?
(d) How long does assembly last ?
(e) How long is the lunch break ?
(f) How long is playtime ?
(g) Do all the lessons get the same amount of time allocated ?
(h) By looking at the pie chart, suggest the time of day when it starts and finishes.

** *If you already know how to use a protractor, you can measure off each eighth in question one as 45°, and in question 2, each individual child gets a 12° segment, so 3 children get 36°.*

101

VENN DIAGRAMS AND SETS

SETS

Any collection of people or things is called a set. You can have a set of tea cups, a set of CD's, a chess set (meaning a set of chess pieces), a set of wheels - in fact a set of anything.

This means that everything in the set is part of the complete set, and belongs there. The important thing about sets is that all the members of the set are the same sort of thing. So you cannot have a soup-dish in a set of tea cups, or a cassette in a set of CD's, or a draught in a chess set.

When we want to show the *name of a set* in mathematics, we put it in curly brackets, like this: $\{\ \}$.

Everything that belongs to a particular set is called a *member* or *element* of the set. In maths we use another sign, like a rather strange *e* to mean *is a member of*, or *is an element of* a set: $\in$.

So we can now write equations like this:

      Franc $\in$ { foreign coins }   meaning: A Franc is a member of the set of 'foreign coins'.

      John $\in$ { boys' names }   meaning: 'John' is a member of the set of 'boy's names'

There is another symbol, with the strange *e* crossed out, which means *is not an element* of a set: $\notin$.

So we can also have an equation like this:

      50 p. $\notin$ { foreign coins } meaning: A 50 p. coin is *not* a member of the set of 'foreign coins'.

      Sarah $\notin$ { boys' names } meaning: 'Sarah' is *not* a member of the set of 'boy's names'.

We can decide on names for sets of particular things.
So if we are given, for example: wood, gas, coal and oil as the members of a set, we can easily see that they are all fuels, and write the equation: wood, gas, coal, oil $\in$ { fuels }

We can also fill in members of a set if we know the set name.
So if we are told to think of members for the set of girls' names, we can immediately think of several, and then write an equation for them: Anne, Jane, Sue, Wendy $\in$ { girls' names }

We can pick out items which do not belong in a set.
So if we are given this list: Birmingham, London, Newcastle, Paris, Leeds, we can immediately spot that Paris is the odd one out (as it is not in England), and we can write two separate equations:
Birmingham, London, Newcastle, Leeds $\in$ { English cities } Paris $\notin$ {English cities}.

Most things you can think of could belong to many different, or overlapping sets:
'Carrot' belongs to the sets: 'vegetables', 'things that grow underground', 'things you can eat', 'orange things', and very many others you can probably think of as well.

Exercise 47

In each of the questions you are given a set of items. What you have to do is think of an appropriate name for each set, and then write the equation correctly. (Like: wood, gas, coal, oil $\in$ { fuels }.

1. coat, tie, shirt, socks
2. oak, elm, beech, ash
3. water, cider, tea, milk
4. Rome, Paris, Madrid, Berlin, Vienna
5. eyes, feet, stomach, elbow
6. shout, bang, grunt, crash, bellow
7. B, J, E, Y, O
8. a, e, i, o, u

Exercise 47 A

In each of these questions you are given the name of the set, and you have to think of four elements that belong to that particular set, and then write the equation. (So if you were given 'girls' names' as the set, you would write (for example): Anne, Jane, Sue, Wendy $\in$ { girls' names } .)

1. colours
2. islands
3. planets
4. wild animals
5. months
6. lessons
7. teachers
8. things I like

Exercise 47 B

In each of these questions, you are given a list of items, one of which does not belong to the particular set. You have to decide which item, and then write out the correct equation for membership of the set, plus the equation for the non-member. (Once again, do it as in the example on the page before : Birmingham, London, Newcastle, Leeds $\in$ { English cities }   Paris $\notin$ {English cities}.)

1. Europe, Asia, Africa, Russia, North America
2. Matthew, Mark, Luke, Mary, John
3. rice, beans, sugar, banana, milk-shake
4. plane, boat, travel, train, car
5. Monday, yesterday, Wednesday, Sunday
6. 0.5, 0.825, $^3/_{10}$, 0.97, 0.04
7. 14, 1, 17, 11, 23, 15
8. 9, 18, 27, 36, 44

Exercise 47 C

Each of the following belongs to more than one set. For each question write down three different sets that it could belong to. Write your answer each time as three separate set equations.

1. kitten
2. man
3. Blackpool
4. William Shakespeare
5. banana
6. 100
7. 7
8. mathematics

Exercise 47 D

Write these set equations out again as sentences in proper English:

1. { things that go bump in the night }
2. house, hut, bungalow, palace $\in$ { dwelling places }
3. Sherlock Holmes, Dr. Watson, Inspector Lestrade, Professor Moriarty $\in$ {fictional characters}   Sir Arthur Conan Doyle $\notin$ {fictional characters}.

103

VENN DIAGRAMS

Venn Diagrams are named after the Rev. John Venn. His idea was to show logical arguments in the form of diagrams, to make them clearer. Venn diagrams are used in mathematics to give information about sets.

The first Venn diagram is very simple. If you want to show a set, you draw a circle or an ellipse (= oval) round it, and label it, usual with a letter.

So, here are two different sets, shown as Venn diagrams:

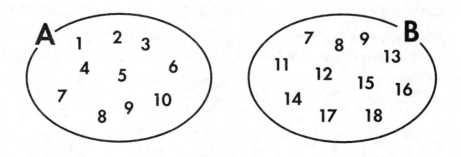

The first ellipse (oval) contains the numerals from one to ten, and has been labelled as Set A.

The second ellipse contains the numerals from seven to eighteen, and has been labelled Set B.

We can write this information as equations, using the brackets which indicate a set:

    Set A = { numerals from one to ten }.
    Set B = { numerals from seven to eighteen }.

When more than one circle or ellipse is shown, as in this case, it is usual to include both (or all) of them inside a rectangle. This represents the universal set. The universal set is the set which contains everything in both (or all of) the sets shown. The universal set also has a special sign, which is a capital **E** done in copperplate handwriting, like this: $\mathscr{E}$.

If you look again at the two sets, A and B, you will notice that there are some numerals which are in both sets. In fact you could say that the two sets overlap. In Venn diagrams, the way we show an overlap is to draw the diagram of the sets precisely so that they do overlap.

In Set A, numerals 1, 2, 3, 4, 5, 6 are not part of the overlap. They do not also come in Set B. So we do not include them in the place where the two ovals overlap each other.

In Set B, numerals 11, 12, 13, 14, 15, 16, 17, 18 are not part of the overlap. They do not also come in Set A. So we do not include them in the place where the two ovals overlap each other.

But the numerals 7, 8, 9, 10 are in both sets. They are where the sets overlap. So we show them in just that place where the two ovals do overlap each other.

Here is the Venn diagram to show what we have just described:

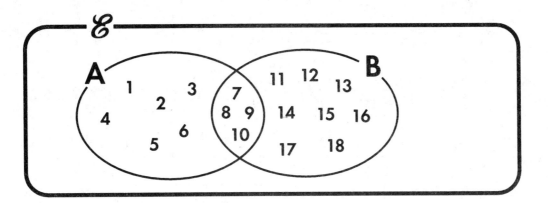

There are some other strange signs or symbols you need to learn to describe the diagram. Firstly there is the **union** of two (or more) sets. The union of two sets is the combination of the two, so it includes *everything* in both of them. There is a special sign for the **union** of sets: $\cup$. This sign for the **union** of sets is sometimes called **cup** (because it looks like a cup).

In our example above: $A \cup B$ = { 1, 2, 3, 4, 5, 6, 7, 8, 9, 10, 11, 12, 13, 14, 15, 16, 17 }.
(You can read this as *A 'cup' B equals ......* or *Union of A and B equals ....* .)

The overlap of the two sets is properly called the intersection. The **intersection** includes all those items which come inside both ellipses, and are therefore part of both sets. There is also a special sign for the intersection of sets: $\cap$. This sign for the intersection is the reverse of the sign for the union, and is sometimes called **cap** (because it looks like a cap).

If we look at the above example: $A \cap B$ = { 7, 8, 9, 10 }.
(You can read this as *A 'cap' B equals ....* or *Intersection of A and B equals ..... .*)

You sometimes see Venn diagrams where there are three or more sets shown, and they may all intersect, or some may intersect and some not. You may also see items which are included in the universal set, but are not in any of the ellipses which show the individual sets.

Here is an example of how you can use Venn diagrams to present information, and to interpret it.

Example (a)

In a group of 100 people, 56 enjoy lemonade, and 65 enjoy milk, while four enjoy neither. Draw a Venn diagram to show this distribution. How many enjoy both lemonade and milk ?

When you come to draw your Venn diagram of this you can show each person as a dot, allocated in his or her correct set.

But first you need to think through what you have got:

(i)   The universal set (which means everyone involved, so it has 100 elements).
(ii)   Set A, the people who like lemonade - 56 elements.
(iii)   Set B, the people who like milk - 65 elements.
(iv)   Four elements which are in the universal set, but not in either A or B.

What we need to work out is how many elements of the two sets A and B belong in the intersection (which is the group of people who like both, in this case).

So, for a start we can exclude the four people who like neither. They can be shown as dots inside the universal set box, but outside the two ellipses for sets A and B.

Now that means that we have only 96 people in the two sets.
But if we add up the totals, $A + B = 56 + 65 = 121$.

We know there are not 121 people. There are only 96. The reason for the greater number is that some people are in both groups - the overlap, or the intersection of the sets.

How many people are in the overlap ? That is simple.
Subtract the real number of people (96) from the sum of the two sets (121) : $121 - 96 = 25$

So there are 25 dots to draw in the intersection of the two sets.

How many do we draw in the rest of the two ellipses ?

Again very simple.
There are 56 people in set A. We have already shown 25 of them in the intersection.
So those left must be $56 - 25 = 31$. We draw 31 dots in the remainder of the ellipse.

There are 65 people in set B. We have already shown 25 of them in the intersection.
So those left must be $65 - 25 = 40$. We draw 40 dots in the remainder of the ellipse.

Here is the resultant Venn diagram:

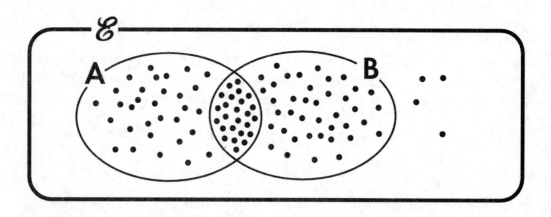

You can check that your Venn diagram fits with the information you are given by simply counting.
There are definitely 56 dots in Set A (including the intersection - that is part of Set A).
There are definitely 65 dots in Set B (including the intersection - that is also part of Set B).
There are four dots outside both sets but in the universal set.
There are 100 dots exactly altogether.

And the answer to the question you were asked: *How many people enjoy both lemonade and milk ?*
is the number of dots in the intersection: 25. Twenty-five people enjoy both.

The following exercises deal with drawing and understanding Venn diagrams. Check back through this section of the topic before you start, and make sure you understand what is involved.

Exercise 48

1.   Draw a Venn diagram to show the following information:

Set A = { 4, 8, 12, 16, 20, 24 }
Set B = { 3, 6, 9, 12, 15, 18, 21, 24 }

Show the intersection of the sets (the part where the two ovals overlap, which contains the numbers that fall in both sets) by colouring it in your diagram.
Which numbers fall in the intersection of the two sets ?

2.   In a group of 45 children, 15 did French, 12 did Technology, and 6 did both subjects.

Draw a Venn diagram to show the above information, and using the diagram, work out how many children did neither subject.
(*Clue: Start by adding the two sets you are given, and subtract the intersection....... .*)

3.   Using the following Venn diagram, answer the questions underneath.

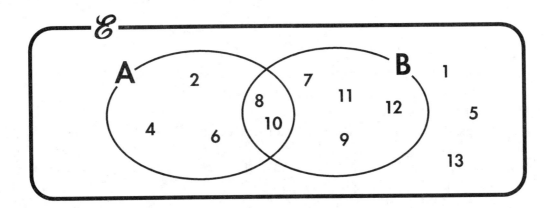

Write down (in the correct form, using the relevant symbols):
(a)   the elements of the universal set
(b)   the elements of Set A
(c)   the elements of Set B
(d)   the intersection of Set A and Set B
(e)   the union of Set A and Set B

(f)   Suggest a name for each of Sets A and B.

4.   A group of people were asked to choose their favourite holiday destination from a choice of: (a) Britain or (b) Europe.
30 said Britain;   20 said Europe; 5 said neither; 15 said both.

Draw a Venn diagram to show the above information.
How many people were asked the question ?

Exercise 48 A Problems

1.   Study the Venn diagram below.
      Set X is the group of people who like egg and bacon for breakfast.
      Set Y is the set of people who like cereals for breakfast.
      Set Z is the group of people who like yoghurt for breakfast.

As you will see, in this diagram there are three sets within the universal set, but you should still be able to work out the questions underneath without any difficulty.

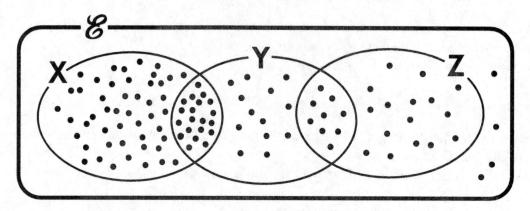

How many elements are there in:
(a)   Set X   (b)   Set Y   (c)   Set Z
(d)   X ∪ Y   (e)   Y ∪ Z   (f)   X ∪ Y ∪ Z
(g)   X ∩ Y   (h)   Y ∩ Z   (i)   X ∩ Z   (j)   ℰ
(k)   How many people like both cereals and eggs and bacon for breakfast ?
(l)   How many people like none of the items ?
(m)   How many people were asked the question ?
(n)   How many people liked both eggs and bacon and yoghurt ?

2.   Certificates for proficiency in sporting events are awarded to a group of children who
      take part in their school year sports competition.
      There are three kinds of certificates: A = Track   B = Field   C = Swimming

            4 children earn certificates in all three.
            4 children earn certificates in both Swimming and Track events.
            5 children earn certificates in both Track and Field events.
            3 children earn certificates in both Swimming and Field events.
            8 earn certificates in Field events only.
            6 earn certificates in Swimming only.
            9 earn certificates in Track events only.
            56 took part but did not earn any certificates.

      (a)   Draw a Venn diagram to show this information.
      (b)   How many children altogether were awarded certificates for each of the following:
                  (i) Track events   (ii) Field events   (iii) Swimming
      (c)   How many children were awarded two or more certificates.
      (d)   How many children altogether won any certificates ?
      (e)   How many children took part altogether ?

In the previous question you should have drawn a diagram rather like the one shown below. If you did not, you will have got the question wrong. Go back to it, and try again with this sort of diagram.

(Clue: Those who won certificates in all three sports belong in the shaded part where all sets intersect.)

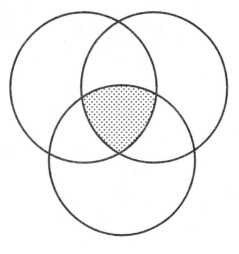

3. Using a layout like the one shown above, draw a Venn diagram to show the following three sets within a universal set of all numbers from one to twelve:

    A = { prime numbers under ten }
    B = { even numbers up to ten }
    C = { three and its multiples up to twelve }

    (a) Which numbers are in the universal set but in none of sets A, B and C ?
    (b) State: (i)   A ∩ B
                     (ii)   B ∩ C
                     (iii) A ∩ C
                     (iv)   A ∩ B ∩ C
         Are any of these intersections vacant ?

4. An outing is arranged for members of a school's rugby, cross-country and hockey teams.

    Three of the rugby team are in the two other teams as well.
    Nine children are in both the rugby and cross-country teams.
    Four of the hockey team are also in the cross-country team, but not the rugby team.
    Five are in the hockey team and the rugby team, but not the cross-country team.
    Three are only in the rugby team, four only in the cross country team, and three only in the hockey team.

    (a) Draw a Venn diagram to show this information.
    (b) Will a coach with thirty seats be large enough to transport them all ?

LINES, ANGLES AND SHAPES

All around you there are examples of lines, angles and shapes. The lines may be straight or curved. The angles may be squared or sharp or blunt. The shapes may be like the ones you have already met, such as squares and rectangles, or they may be other regular shapes, or they may be irregular. Most man-made things have regular shapes, but so do many in nature, from snowflakes to the cells of bees.

In this topic we deal with regular geometric shapes, and all the lines in them are straight.

A straight line is the shortest distance between two points.

When two lines join they form an angle.

When a series of lines joins at different points they enclose a shape.

ANGLES

When two lines meet at a point to form an angle, it is possible to measure the space between the two lines. It is the size of this opening between the lines that is the measurement of the angle.
The measurement of an angle has nothing to do with the lengths of the lines projecting from the point.

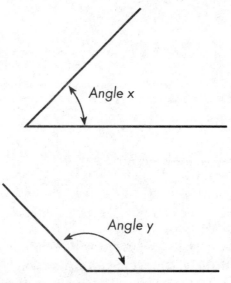

In this diagram you can see two different angles, one with quite a small space between the lines, one with a much larger space.

We use a protractor to measure angles, and we measure them in degrees, which are shown by a small circle above the line following the number ($^{\circ}$). A diagram of the protractor and how to use it is shown on the following page. You will need to get one of your own for this topic.

When you have to draw angles, or lines or shapes, in your exercise book, always draw them in pencil, using a sharpened pencil and a ruler. Do not draw them thickly and heavily, but draw them clearly enough to be seen.

Types of Angles

Angles are named in the following way according to their sizes:

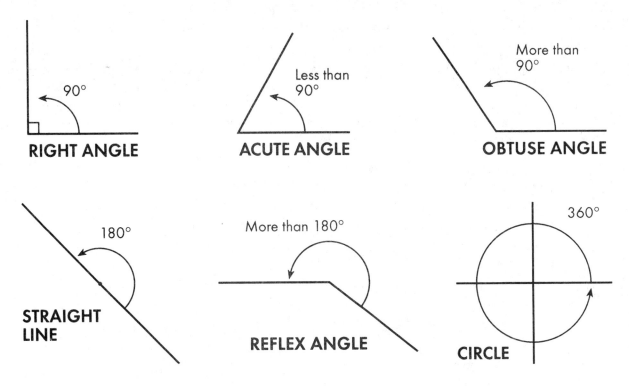

Look carefully at this diagram.

The **right angle** (90°) is a quarter of a turn. If you were turning a full circle, and you stopped at 90° you would be a quarter of the way round. Right angles are very familiar to us.
They are the measurement of most corners. They are the angles of all squares and rectangles.
Notice that a right angle is usually shown by a little square inside it.
Other angles are often shown with a curve in them (but not with an arrow on), to indicate the turn.

The **acute angle** is any angle less than a right angle (less than 90°).

The **obtuse angle** is any angle more than one right angle but less than two right angles (more than 90° but less than 180°).

The **straight line** does not look like an angle, but in a way it is. A right angle is a quarter of a turn. If you go on turning, until you are facing the exact opposite direction from where you started, you have completed a 180° degree turn. If you were drawing it as two arms of an angle, the result would be a straight line. You can also describe this as two right angles.

The **reflex angle** is an angle greater than 180° but less than 360° . So if you were turning, you would continue past the straight line stage, and carry on. This means that you have done more than a half turn (or more than two right angles).

The **circle**, or complete turn is 360°, or four right angles. After you have turned a complete circle, you are back facing the same way as when you started. In the diagram the four right angles of the complete revolution have been marked.

The Protractor

In order to understand this section, and the whole topic, you need to buy a protractor.
They are quite small, usually shaped like a half circle and made of transparent plastic.
The outer rim is divided into 180 equal parts. This is the number of degrees in a half revolution (revolution = turn), so each division is one degree.
There is also an inner circle of divisions, numbered from 1 to 180, but these start at the opposite side, and go round in the opposite direction.

It is very easy to decide which of these two scales to use in measuring your angle, as explained in the following instructions for the use of the protractor:

(i)   Place the base line of the protractor on the lower arm of the angle.
(ii)   Find where the other arm lies on the protractor scales.
(iii)   Use whichever scale **starts at zero** - not the one that starts at 180.
(iv)   Count the degrees shown for the angle.

Here is a diagram of a protractor, showing how it works:

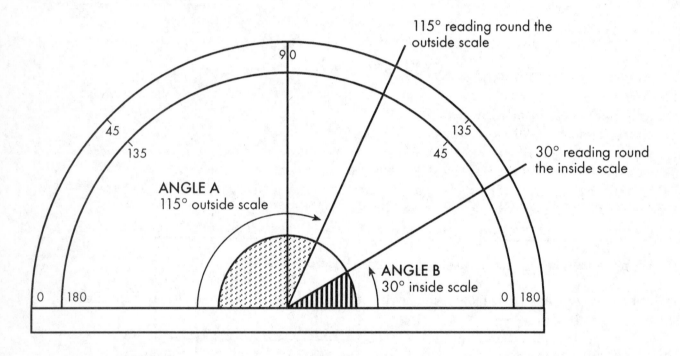

As you can see, there are two angles shown.

Angle A is a reflex angle, and the turning direction is from the left hand side of the page. (We could describe the turn as clockwise - in the same direction as a clock.) We look for the zero where the angle starts - on the bottom left side, and we find that it is on the outside scale, so we read round to where the arm of the angle crosses the scale on the rim of the protractor, and read off the figure in degrees - 115 °.

Angle B is an acute angle, and the turning direction is from the right hand side of the page (which is anticlockwise). We find the scale which has a a zero on the bottom right side where the angle starts, find it is the inside scale this time, and we read round until the arm of the angle crosses the scale (not the rim where the outer scale is, but the inside scale), and read off the figure in degrees - 30 °.

SHAPES

You have already seen some shapes in *Topic Ten* and *Topic Eleven*, which dealt with perimeter and area. These shapes were the square and the rectangle. You may want to look back to page 60 where they were first introduced.

Here are their definitions again:

A square is a four sided regular shape in which all the sides are of equal length, and all the angles are right angles.

A rectangle is a four-sided regular shape in which the opposite sides are of equal length, and all the angles are right angles.

What is added to the definitions here is the fact that in each case all the angles are right angles.

The most common of the other regular shapes you may meet is the triangle. Here is its definition:

A triangle has three sides and three angles.

This is very simple indeed. Triangles can come in all sizes, and with various angles.
One special triangle is the *right angled triangle*, where one of its three angles is a right angle.

The angles of a triangle added together always come to 180°.
So if you know two angles of a triangle, you can always work out the third. (Add the two angles you know, and subtract the result from 180° .)
This is the formula: $180° - (\angle A + \angle B) = \angle C$

Notice the useful symbol $\angle$, which means *angle*.

Here is a diagram to remind you of the three shapes you know about:

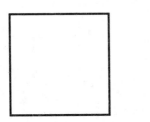

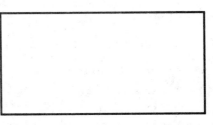

SQUARE (4 sides, all sides equal, 4 right angles)

RECTANGLE (4 sides, opposite sides equal, 4 right angles)

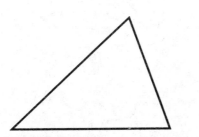

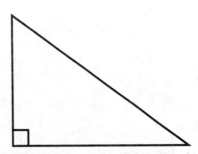

TRIANGLE (three sides, three angles, angles add up to 180°)

RIGHT ANGLED TRIANGLE (one of the three angles is a right angle)

Exercise 49

The questions in this exercise are all to do with the following diagram, which shows eight angles:

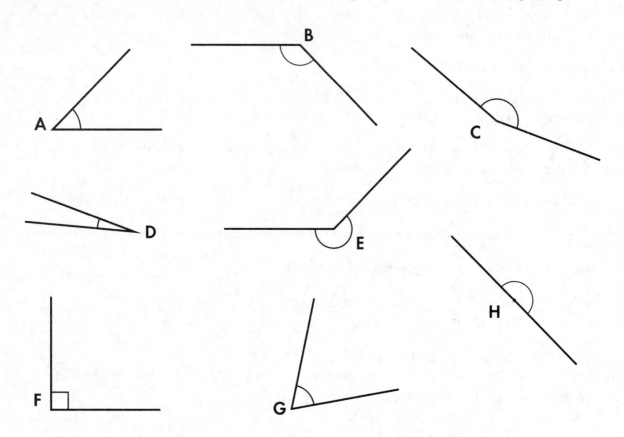

1. Copy out the angles in the diagram (each labelled with its correct letter) in order of their size, starting with the smallest angle, and finishing with the largest angle.

2. For each angle shown, write its letter and the correct name for that sort of angle.

3. Using a protractor, measure each of the angles.

4. Draw the following angles (using pencil and ruler but not protractor):

    (a)   an acute angle smaller than ∠ A
    (b)   an obtuse angle smaller than ∠ B
    (c)   a reflex angle larger than ∠ E.

Exercise 49 A

1. How many degrees are there in the following:
    (a)   a right angle   (b) a straight line   (c)   a circle

2. Give the correct names for angles of the following sizes:
    (a)   12°   (b)   120°   (c)   195°   (d)   180°   (e)   90° .

3. What sort of angle is formed by two right angles ?

4. What sort of angle is formed by three right angles ?

5. How many right angles are there in:
    (a)   a straight line   (b)   a circle   (c)   an angle of 45° .

114

Exercise 49 B

1. Using a pencil, ruler and protractor, draw the following angles:

    (a) 50° (b) 130° (c) 65° (d) 125° (e) 5°

    (f) 27° (g) 119° (h) 11° (i) 90° (j) 180° .

2. Write the correct name for each angle you have drawn in questions (a) to (j)
    for Number 1 above.

3. Using a pencil, ruler and protractor, draw the following angles:

    (a) 195° (b) 250° (c) 294° (d) 270° (e) 345°

Exercise 49 C

1. Carefully measure with a protractor each angle of each of the following triangles.
    Note down the measurements, and add them up to make sure the total does come to 180°.

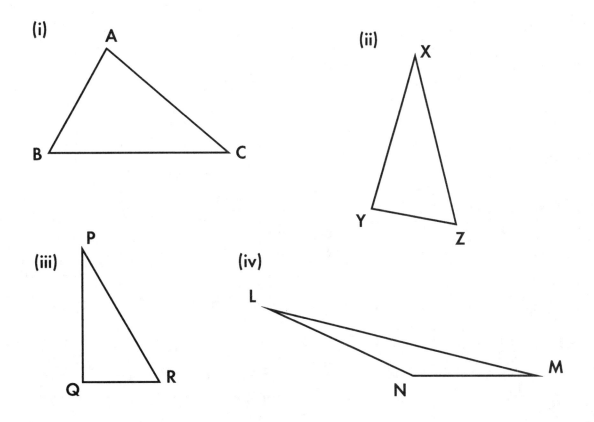

2. (a) What is the sum of the angles of a triangle ?
    (b) What is the sum of the angles of a rectangle ?

3. Draw the following triangles (you may make their sides as long or short as you wish) :
    (i) $\angle A = 30°$, $\angle B = 70°$, $\angle C = 80°$.
    (ii) $\angle X = 60°$, $\angle Y = 30°$, $\angle Z = 90°$.

4. You are given two of the three measurements for the angles of a triangle.
    Calculate the third angle.
    (i) $\angle A = 50°$, $\angle B = 90°$, $\angle C = ?$
    (ii) $\angle X = 20°$, $\angle Y = 130°$, $\angle Z = ?$.

115

CIRCLES

A circle is a round plane figure. (Plane means flat or two-dimensional.) Its outside, is called the circumference. The circumference is the same distance from the centre at any point.

Here is a diagram to show the different parts of a circle and their names:

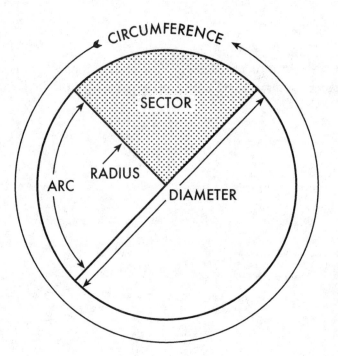

Here is a simplified statement of the meaning of the different terms:

CIRCUMFERENCE	The outside edge of the circle
RADIUS	The distance from the centre to the circumference. (*Plural:* radii)
DIAMETER	The distance across the circle from edge to edge through the centre
CENTRE	The midpoint of the circle, equally distant from any point on the edge
ARC	Any part of the circumference cut off by two radii
SECTOR	A piece of the inside of a circle contained within two radii

To draw a circle accurately you need a good compass, and a sharp pencil fitted in it.

To draw a circle of a given radius, you must measure it out with a ruler. Place the point of the compass on the mark for zero units, and open the compass to place the pencil point on the figure for the radius you have been given. Take care not to change the opening of the compass when you draw the circle.

To draw a circle of a given diameter, you must open your compass to **half** the figure given for the diameter. This might sound strange but if you think about it, and look at the diagram on the page before, you will see that a diameter is two radii.

This is quite a useful rule about circles, and you can remember it by two formulae:

D = 2R (Diameter equals twice the radius.)

$R = {}^{D}/_{2}$ (Radius equals diameter divided by two, *or* half the diameter)

Example (a)

Draw a circle of diameter 8 cm.

Firstly notice that you are given the diameter not the radius.

Take your ruler and compass. Place the compass point on the zero cm. mark on the ruler, and open the compass till the pencil point rests on the 4 cm. line.

It is 4 cm. not 8 cm. because your compass marks out the radius not the diameter. To find the radius you must halve the diameter.

Take care not to change the radius as you draw the circle. Check it by measuring across the circle through the centre (shown by the little mark left on the page by the compass point) from one side of the circumference to the other. It should measure 8 cm.

As a practice, now try to draw circles of *diameter* 8 cm., 10 cm., 6 cm., 5 cm., and 3 cm. for yourself.

FINDING THE CIRCUMFERENCE OF A CIRCLE

It is easy to measure straight lines, but it is much harder to measure round curves. Take various circular shapes like coins or the tops of tins, and try measuring round them with your ruler. You will find that the ruler slips and slides and you are never sure where you started and where to stop. If two or more people try to measure the same object (especially a very small one like a coin) they often get different results.

In fact it is not even very easy to measure the diameter of a circular object, because you cannot be quite sure where the middle is. Here is a clever way of measuring the diameter of a circular shape with the help of two set squares:

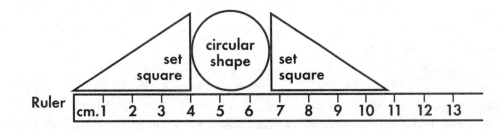

The set squares transfer the diameter of the circle down onto the ruler. If you follow down the side of the first set square you come out at the 4 cm. mark, and the second set square brings you to the 7 cm. mark on the ruler. So the circle in between the two has a diameter of 7 cm. - 4 cm. = 3 cm.

Try this method for yourself with the circular shapes you have collected.

Now here is a practical method of measuring the circumference of a circle:

Take a round shape (like a coin or tin lid), and make a clear mark anywhere on the circumference. Then place the shape next to a ruler, with the mark level with the zero line on the ruler. Then roll the shape along the ruler edge until the mark is facing directly down again. This means the circle has made one complete turn. All of its edge (circumference) has therefore been used. See what measurement on the ruler the mark is now pointing to. That is the measurement of the circumference of that circular shape. Here is a diagram to show you how it works:

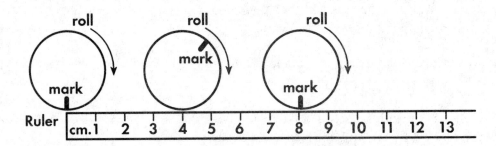

Try this with all the circular objects you have collected, measuring their diameter by the ruler and set squares method, and their circumference by the rolling method. Make a table like this:

SHAPE	DIAMETER	CIRCUMFERENCE
Plate	10 cm.	32 cm.
Sellotape reel	8 cm.	25 cm.
Base of drink can	4 cm	12.5 cm.
Tin lid	3 cm.	9.5 cm.
Coin (1)	22 mm.	70 mm
Coin (2)	25 mm.	80 mm.

See how your measurements of circular objects compare with the above table.
Can you guess what coin (1) and coin (2) in the table were ?

Have you noticed the connection between the diameter and the circumference ? Try multiplying each figure you have for the diameter by three. You will discover that the circumference is just a little more than the result of your multiplication.

In fact the circumference of a circle is roughly 3.142 times the diameter. Or we can write it as $3\frac{1}{7}$ times the diameter. Neither of these figures is exactly right. The real figure is a strange number that goes on with decimal points forever. It is called **pi** and is named after a Greek letter that looks like this: π
You will learn more about it when you go on to the next Keystage.

ARCS AND SECTORS

Look back at the diagram on page 144. You will see the two labels: *arc* and *sector* shown on the circle, and the definitions of what they are stated underneath.

We can mark off arcs of a circle, or draw sectors of a circle to a given size by using a method of measurement which we have already learnt. Turn back to *Topic 22* (page 110), and read about measuring angles. In particular check the section about the use of a protractor on page 112. We measure arcs of a circle in degrees, and we draw the angles for them using a protractor.

Firstly draw the circle, make a small mark to show the centre, and then from it mark in any line from centre to circumference. This is a radius.
Place your protractor along the radius you have drawn, and mark the point for the number of degrees of arc you want to show. Join the centre of the circle to your mark. (If it is beyond the edge of the circle, you can rub out the part on the outside; if it does not reach the edge, carefully extend the line till it does.) You now have an arc of the required measurement on the circumference, and the two radii enclose a sector of that angle.

Look at the example to see how it works:

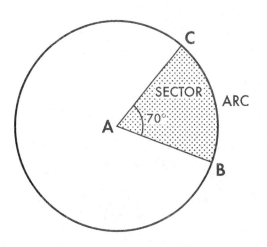

Exercise 50

1. Draw circles of radius: (a)   3 cm.   (b)   25 mm   (c)   4.2 cm.
2. Draw circles of diameter: (a)   4 cm.   (b)   56 mm.   (c)   8.4 cm.
3. Using the same centre point, draw three circles of radius 0.8 cm., 13 mm. and 2.1 cm.
4. If a circle has a radius of 3.9 cm. what will its diameter be ?
5. If a circle has a diameter of 18.6 cm., what will its radius be ?
6. Using the methods shown above, measure the diameter and circumference of a 2p. coin.
7. A circle has a diameter of 2.6 cm. Will its circumference be roughly:
    (a)   5 cm.   (b)   6.5 cm.   (c)   8 cm.
8. A circle has a radius of 10 mm. Will its circumference be roughly:
    (a)   31 mm.   (b)   62 mm.   (c)   124 mm.
9. Draw a circle of radius 30 mm., and mark on it by shading a sector of angle 45 $^\circ$.
10. Draw a circle of diameter 10 cm., and mark on its circumference an arc of 110 $^\circ$.

SYMMETRY

A shape has symmetry when it can be cut in half by a line, and the two halves match each other exactly. This line about which the shape can be "folded" is called the line or axis of symmetry, and the two halves of the shape are said to be symmetrical.

Some shapes have more than one axis of symmetry. This means they can be cut into identical halves in several different ways. For example, a rectangle has two lines of symmetry, one running along its length, and the other across its width. But a square has four lines of symmetry, and a circle has endless lines of symmetry, because every single diameter (the lines running through the centre from edge to edge) is one. Have a look at the following diagrams, and you will see how lines of symmetry work:

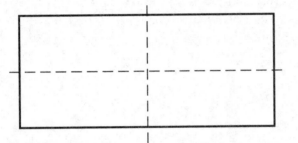

RECTANGLE - two lines of symmetry

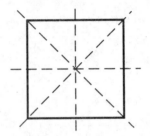

SQUARE - four lines of symmetry

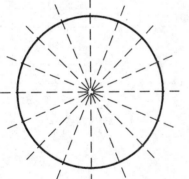

CIRCLE -
only a few
of the very
many lines
of symmetry
have been
shown

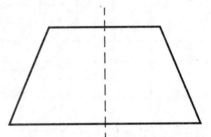

This shape has only one
line of symmetry

Exercise 51

1.   Make a list of flat objects, and next to each write whether it is symmetrical or not symmetrical. If it is symmetrical, say how many lines of symmetry you think it has. (Some things to include in your list might be: ruler, set-square, protractor, a page of your book and coins (including some like the 20 p. and 50 p. which are not round).

2.   Draw the first ten letters of the alphabet in large size. (You will find it helps if you draw them on squared paper, so that they are done accurately). For each one write down whether it is symmetrical or not symmetrical, and draw any lines of symmetry you can find on it.   *continued*

3.   Copy the following shapes onto squared paper. (One centimetre squared paper is best if you have any.) Draw in all the lines of symmetry you can find.

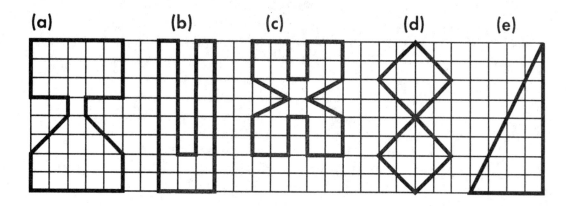

4.   Here you are given three half shapes (a, b and c) and one quarter shape (d), together with the lines of symmetry that divide them. Copy them onto squared paper and complete the symmetrical shapes, by filling in the missing parts.

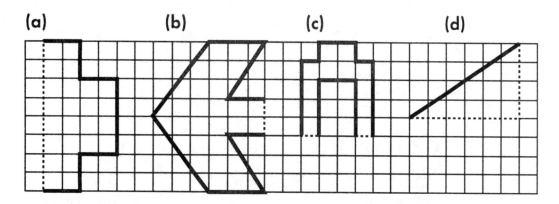

OTHER SYMMETRIES

The symmetry we have been looking at might be called folding symmetry. In it you can fold a shape along its line of symmetry, and the two halves will exactly overlap.

There are two other sorts of symmetry. The first of these is called **Reflective symmetry**. You know what a reflection is. It is what you see in a mirror. If you hold the page of a book up to a mirror, you will see that all the writing is backwards. This is because mirror images are reversed. (Try holding up your right hand while looking in a mirror. The image of you has held up its hand on the left side !)

Reflective symmetry is when a shape or part of a shape has a mirror image of itself. The line of symmetry is where you put the mirror to create the reverse shape; we could call it the mirror line.

Look at the diagram on page 122 to see how this works. The two shapes are the mirror image of each other. Then try it yourself. See if you can draw two simple shapes of your own, one of which is the mirror image of the other. If you can get a small hand mirror and can place it on the line of symmetry (the mirror line) it will help you.

This diagram shows two shapes which have reflective symmetry. This means that shape (b) is the mirror image of shape (a). Hold the page up to a mirror. What do you see ?

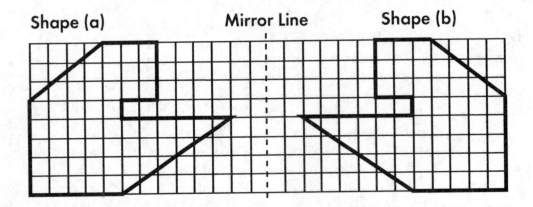

Shape (a)   Mirror Line   Shape (b)

The other kind of symmetry you need to know about is called **Rotational symmetry**.
Rotational symmetry is when a shape can be turned or rotated about its own centre, and still appears the same. Look at the following shapes:

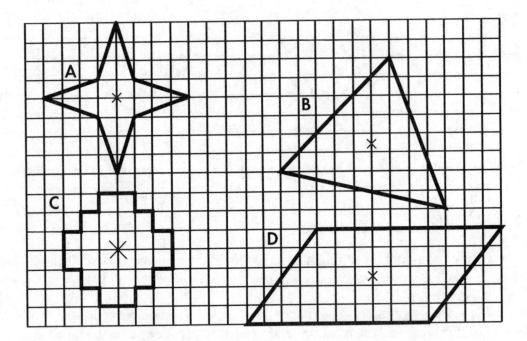

All of the shapes shown in this diagram have rotational symmetry, but some have what might be called better rotational symmetry. Try this practical exercise:

Trace each shape onto a piece of paper. Cut out your tracing of each shape and lay it on top of the one in the book. Then turn it slowly round until it fits again. If you have to turn it a complete circle, than it does not have rotational symmetry. But if you get a match before turning all the way round, then the shape does have rotational symmetry. For each shape, see how many times you get a perfect match when turning through the circle. (This number is called the *order* of rotational symmetry it has.)

Exercise 51 A

1 (a)   Which of the following letters are symmetrical:

Q   R   S   T   U   V   W   X   Y   Z

1 (b)   Which of them has more than one line of symmetry ?

1 (c)   Which of them (if any) have reflective symmetry ?

2.   How many lines of symmetry are there in
         (a)   a square   (b)   a rectangle   (c)   a regular oval shape
         (d)   a triangle of which all the sides are equal
         (e)   a triangle of which all the sides have different lengths
         (f)   a triangle with two sides of equal length

3.   Copy these diagrams of symmetrical shapes onto a sheet of (squared) paper and draw
        in the missing pieces. (The lines of symmetry are shown by the dotted lines.)

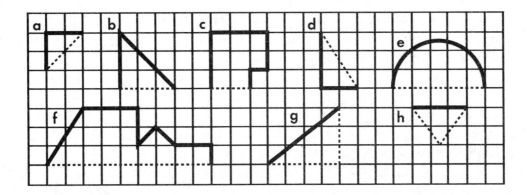

4.   Draw a shape of your own which has two lines of symmetry

5.   Draw a shape of your own and then draw a second shape which is reflectively symmetrical
        to it. (You should certainly use squared paper if possible for this question.)

6.   Draw a shape of your own which has four degrees of rotational symmetry.

123

PROBABILITY

Probability means the chance of an event happening - how probable it is.
It is possible to assess the probability of an event using maths.

Example (a)

(i)   Having an ice cream now

You have to choose between *YES* and *NO* for the probability of this event. Since you are doing maths, you are probably very unlikely to have an ice cream right now. So you would answer NO.

(ii)   Having an ice-cream ever

Unless you dislike or are not allowed ice-cream, there is a very good chance that you will have an ice-cream some time in your life. So this time the probability will be YES.

Notice how important time scale is to the assessment of probability. The more specific the time, the lower the probability, while over a longer time, the probability increases - the event becomes more likely. This is often an important factor in working out probability.

Exercise 52

For each of the following statements, assess the probability of each event by simply writing **YES** or **NO**, depending on whether the event is **probable** or **not probable**.

1.	Falling asleep tonight	2.	Spending 10 p. or more today
3.	Going to the moon this year	4.	Becoming Prime-Minister
5.	Swimming the English Channel	6.	Running away from school
7.	Going to school during this week	8.	Not eating again today
9.	Reading a whole story book today	10.	Getting a good mark for this exercise.

So far we have looked at simple *YES/NO* divides into probable and not probable. We have seen how the time scale of the event can help us decide on the answer. There are many other factors to consider.

In *Exercise 50* above, the normal answer to *Question Three* would be NO. Why ? Because there are many considerations which make it improbable. You are not an astronaut. You are probably a boy or girl - and there have been no child missions to the moon yet. There are no moon missions going on the moment. You have plenty of information. The NO answer is almost certain.

Question Five might not produce such a definite NO. A fine swimmer, already in training, and likely to do very well in the sport could write YES. The majority of people, however, would still write NO.

In the case of *Question Seven* - for those doing the exercise at school, the YES answer is absolutely certain, and NO is impossible. But there may well be people doing the exercise at home in the middle of the school holidays, or off sick; there may be adults doing it, who do not go to school at all.

As you can see from looking at these questions, probability is assessed by taking into account a whole range of factors which influence the event. We can make a list of them, on each side of the question. We can also expect very different lists for different people.

Example (b)

Getting a good school report

For this event, two children in the same class might provide the opposite answer on the YES/NO choice. Both of them would be right in their answer, because in each case the factors to be considered would be different. Compare them in the following table of reasons by two such children:

Brenda Brainy	**Fred Foolish**
YES	**NO**
I always get a good report	I have never had a good report
I work hard at all my lessons	I only work hard at football
I am amazingly clever	I am not too bright (except in football)
I am good at exams	I hate exams (and there isn't one in football)
I have an excellent memory	I cannot always remember my own name
The teachers all like me	Only the games teacher likes me

Exercise 52 A

In this exercise, you once again have to assess the probability as *YES* or *NO*, but for each question you must also write a list of reasons, on the same basis as those given above, for your answer.

1.   Going abroad on holiday this year   2.   Having chips for lunch tomorrow
3.   Playing cricket for England one day   4.   Improving your maths
5.   Learning to speak Spanish   6.   Visiting a relative this year
7.   Working harder in school   8.   Going to university
9.   Enjoying your school lunch at least once this week
10.   Being sent to see the head-teacher of your school some time this month.

If you are doing the exercise in school, or with other people, compare your answers and the different factors which led you to reach them.

We have now seen very clearly that probability depends on a wide variety of factors. What this means in reality is that probability can rarely be as simple as a *YES/NO* division. These are the two extremes. In most judgements about probability, the most likely answer is **MAYBE**. We might well go on to add the words: " It all depends on............." , and follow them with a list of influencing factors, or at least state one very important factor.

In fact there are numerous different levels of probability between a real *YES* (absolute certainty of happening) and a real *NO* (absolute certainty of not happening). We can think of probability as a sort of sliding scale, and the chance of something happening as a percentage or fraction.
(Check back to Topic 15 on page 80 if you are not sure about percentages.)

If there is no chance of something happening, it obviously will not happen.
If something is absolutely certain, then it obviously will happen.
Right in the middle is an even chance. The event is just as likely to happen as not to happen.
We often call this a fifty-fifty chance.

So our probability scale might look something like this:

0	$\frac{1}{2}$	1
0%	50%	100%
No chance	Even Chance	Certain

Exercise 52 B

We can use the sort of scale shown above to decide probability. In this exercise, you have to decide on the probability of events. You can give them three different probabilities. If there is no chance enter the probability as zero, if the event is certain enter it as 1, if it is an even chance enter it as $\frac{1}{2}$.

1. You will attend your school for ordinary lessons next Sunday.
2. You will have something to drink within the next twelve hours.
3. If you have a race with another boy or girl, you will be the winner.
4. When two children have a race one of them will win.
5. A boy will be better at maths than a girl.
6. The next baby born in any family will be a girl.
7. It is raining somewhere in the world at the moment.
8. It will rain somewhere in Britain tomorrow.
9. If we toss a coin once we will get a head.
10. If we toss a coin a very large number of times, we will get more heads than tails.

Most people doing this exercise will have come up with two zeros, three ones, and five halves.
Some of the questions really do have only one right answer. Others depend on the person answering and on other factors which may affect it. Try to work out which of your answers *must* be correct.

Inserting the fifty-fifty or half marker in the middle of the scale has given us a better measure of probability than just a plain YES/NO response. However, we do not have to stop at just the addition even chance marker. We can put in others as well. Two more have been inserted on the following scale:

0	$\frac{1}{4}$	$\frac{1}{2}$	$\frac{3}{4}$	1
0%	25%	50%	75%	100%
No chance	Unlikely	Even Chance	Likely	Certain

This sort of scale represents much more closely the situation in the real world, where we are not so concerned with things which are absolutely certain either to happen or not to happen, and need to make judgements about the probability of things which may or may not happen.

So you may be fairly sure that you have passed your English exam, but you may well not be quite certain. So you could give it a 75% probability. You may well think you could have come top in the exam. It is not all that likely, but it is possible, so you might give it a 25% probability. Answers will depend on the people involved. Brenda Brainy (from *example (b)* on page 117) might give the probability of doing her homework as 100%, while Fred Foolish would only rate it at 25%. On the other hand he might say that there was a 75% chance he would play football after school, while Brenda would rate that at zero.

In the following exercise, there are just such variations depending on who is answering and, of course, on the circumstances involved.

Exercise 52 C

Give the probability of the following events as zero, 25%, 50%, 75% or 100%:

1. You can count to 100 in less than 30 seconds.
2. You will meet someone who is not a family member next Sunday.
3. You will play a ball game of one sort or another today.
4. You will get into trouble at school some time this month.
5. You will feel hungry within the next two hours.
6. Your best friend will talk to you today.
7. The next person you see will be a girl.
8. You will lose some money some time this year.
9. You will go to sleep before 10 o'clock tonight.
10. You will stay at school until you are at least eighteen.

Exercise 52 D

Now write down the MAIN factor or factors which made you decide on your answer for each of the questions in *Exercise 50 C*. For some you may need to give a complicated explanation, and many things may have been taken into account. Some may have only one key factor.

As you will probably have realised, it is possible to insert many more points on the scale. We might say that something very likely indeed but not absolutely certain had a 90% probability (0.9 or $^9/_{10}$ on a scale of zero to one). Something that was close to an even chance, but perhaps a little more likely to happen than not to happen could be given a 60% probability (0.6 or $^6/_{10}$), while something that was really very unlikely indeed, but still possible might get 10% (0.1 or $^1/_{10}$).

The problem with this approach is that we are really guessing at an exact figure. Is something 60% likely to happen, or is the probability really closer to 70% ? It is hard to say without a proper method.

There is a mathematical method of working out the probability of a specific event occurring, to give an exact figure, rather than just a good guess. You need to learn the following formula:

Probability $=$ **The number of ways an event could happen**
The total possible number of events

So to find probability, you have to find out the number of different possible ways an event could take place, and then **divide** this figure by the total number of events. Look at the following example to see how this works:

Example (c)

*There is a pack of ten pieces of card. Each card has a number written on one side. The numbers on the cards run from one to ten. What is the probability of picking out a card with an **even** number ?*

(i)   How many ways could the event happen ?
        The event is picking an even-numbered card. There are five even numbers: 2, 4, 6, 8, 10.
        So there are five different ways we can pick an even number.
        This gives us the top line of the formula as 5.

(ii)   What is the total possible number of events ? The total number of cards is ten.
        So we can pick a card ten times (after which there are none left).
        That gives us the bottom line of the formula: 10

(ii)   We can now write out the equation:

        Probability   =   The number of ways an event could happen
                            The total possible number of events

        P   = $\frac{5}{10}$ (five divided by ten)   = $^1/_2$

        So the probability of picking an even-number card is a half (or 0.5, or 50%).

Exercise 52 E is a set of questions about the same pack of card as described in this example.

Exercise 52 E

You have a pack of ten cards numbered from one to ten, as in the example. For each of the questions, you have to work out the probability of the specified event occurring.

1.   What is the probability of choosing a card with an odd number ?

2.   What is the probability of choosing a card with a number between one and five inclusive ?

3.   What is the probability of choosing a card with the number three ?

4.   What is the probability of choosing a card with either of the numbers 2 and 3 ?

5.   What is the probability of choosing a card with any of the numbers 4, 5 and 6 ?

You could make a pack of cards like this one. Try drawing a card 100 times, and seeing how often odd and even numbers, and each number separately comes up. If you go on and do the experiment several hundred times you will find the results come much closer to the mathematical probability.

AN INTRODUCTION TO ALGEBRA

Algebra is a mathematical method of solving problems. It works by using letters for the things we are trying to work out. If you think about it, in any problem you are trying to calculate an *unknown* - an unknown amount, or distance or quantity. What algebra does is construct a sum (which is properly called an equation) in which letters are used for the unknown. These letters are known as 'symbolic numbers'.

We can also use letters to stand in for numbers. We can then allocate the letters particular values, which will give different results to the equation they are part of. Letters used in this way are known as 'variables'. Look at these two examples to show you how letters are used in these ways:

Example (a)

Three villages, Dullminster, Boringham and Yawnsville, lie on a straight road. The distance from Dullminster to Boringham is x kilometres. The distance from Boringham to Yawnsville is twice that distance. Construct algebraic equations for the distances between the three villages.

This sounds very complicated. But what it means is this: *Make up sums using letters instead of numbers to show the distances between the villages.*

Well we know the first one; The question tells you that Dullminster to Boringham is x km.

The question also tells you that Boringham to Yawnsville is twice that. What is twice x ? Well we could write it as $x + x$ km. We could also write it as 2 x x km.

Now what about Dullminster to Yawnsville ? Well the first bit of the journey (as far as Boringham) is x km. The second bit (Boringham to Yawnsville) is $x + x$ km. So altogether we seem to have three times km. We could write it as $x + x + x$ km. Or we could write it as 3 x x km.

The x in these equations is a symbolic number. It stands for an unknown quantity.

Example (b)

Three villages, Dullminster, Boringham and Yawnsville, lie on a straight road. The distance from Dullminster to Boringham is x kilometres. The distance from Boringham to Yawnsville is twice that distance. If $x = 7$ km., what are the distances between each village ?

We have our three old villages again, but this time there is some more information. We know what x stands for. When we are given a value for a symbol, we can carry out a process called 'translation' or 'substitution'. This means we write down our algebraic equations (the simple sums with x in them that we worked out in the first example), and then replace the x's with the real number. We can then work out the actual distances.

Our first task is to fill in the real value (7 km.) in place of all those x's:

Dullminster to Boringham	=	x km.	=	7 km.		
Boringham to Yawnsville	=	$x + x$ km.	=	$7 + 7$ km.	=	14 km.
Dullminster to Yawnsville	=	$x + x + x$ km.	=	$7 + 7 + 7$ km.	=	21 km.

We have used the letter x in these examples. You can of course use any letter. Quite often there will be two or more unknowns in a problem, each with its own letter. Here is an example using two unknowns, and showing you how we can use the value of one to get to the value of the other:

Example (c)

Bell ran a km. and Elston ran b km. The total distance they ran was 35 km. If $a = 19$, how far did Elston run ?

The first thing to do is make up our algebraic equation - the sum: $a + b = 35$ km.
The next thing is to do our translating. We know the value of a, so we substitute that value for a :

$$19 \text{ km.} + b = 35 \text{ km.}$$

Now, what must you add to 19 to make 35 ? As you can see, simply take 19 from 35, and you have the answer: $35 - 19 = 16$. And that is the value of b . Check it by adding the values of a and b : 19 km. $+ 16$ km. $= 35$ km. So Elston ran 16 km.

See how you get on now with this simple exercise using letters for numbers.

Exercise 53

1. A box weighs x kg. How much will five such boxes weigh ?
2. A box weighs x kg. If $x = 4$, how much does the box weigh ?
3. A box weighs x kg. If $x = 6$, how much will three such boxes weigh ?
4. In a test, Bill got y marks, and Ben got twice as many. What did Ben get ?
5. In a test, Bill got y marks. If y stands for 7, what did he get ?
6. In a test, Bill got y marks, and Ben got twice as many. If y is 6, what did Ben get ?
7. It takes me an hour to run p miles. How far can I run in two hours, at the same speed ?
8. If I can run p miles in an hour, how far can I run at the same speed in three hours, if p is 7 ?
9. One box weighs x kg., and another box weighs y kg. What do the two boxes weigh ?
10. One box weighs x kg., and another weighs y kg. If x is 3 and y is 4, what is the weight of the two boxes together ?
11. One box weighs x kg., and another weighs y kg. If x is 5, and the total weight of the boxes is 15 kg., what is the weight of the other box ?
12. One box weighs x kg., and another weighs y kg. If x is 3, and y is twice x , what is the total weight of the two boxes ?

Simplifying

It is always a good idea to make things as simple as possible. In algebra this is often done by putting **like terms** together with each other.

Suppose we have: $x + x + x + x$. This is a very clumsy way of writing things down. What is actually there ? Four x 's. This is very obvious. If we had $2 + 2 + 2 + 2$, we would call it four twos, and we could write it as 4 x 2.

In algebra the way of writing four x's is even easier, because we leave out the multiplication sign, and write it just as we say it: four x's = $4x$; three y's = $3y$; seven a's = $7a$;

We can even do it with two unknowns: x *number of* y's = xy.

When we simplify we collect all the like terms together. We collect all the x's and all the y's , and all the xy's as well, and put them together.

So if we have $x + x + x - x$, we can see that there are three x's minus one x : $2x$ altogether. If we have $2x + x + 3x - 4x$, we can see that there are two plus one plus three x's (six x's altogether) minus four x : $6x - 4x = 2x$.

We might have x's and y's all mixed up: $2x - 4x + 3y + 3x - y + 2xy$.
The way to handle this is take each term in turn. First the x's: $2x - 4x + 3x = x$.
Next we can deal with the y's : $3y - y = 2y$.
Finally we have a mixed term, all by itself: $2xy$. (Do not try to combine mixed terms which have two unknowns in them with terms which have a single unknown.)

So now we can write out the simplified equation: $x + 2y + 2xy$.

This sort of algebra is really like a game or puzzle. In the following exercise, see if you can sort out the terms and simplify the expressions in the same way.

Exercise 54

1. $2x + 4x$
2. $3a - a + 2a$
3. $z + 2z + 3z - 5z$
4. $2x - 3x + 3y + 2x$
5. $2f + 3e + f - e$
6. $p - 2p + 3q + 3p - q + 2p$
7. $5x + 3y - 4x - 3y + y + 2xy.$
8. $4a + 6b - ab$
9. $3r - 2rs + 6s - rs - s$
10. $2x - 3y - 2xy + 3y + 2xy - 2x$

Did you spot the two trick questions ? One of them cannot be simplified (so the answer is the same as the question). In another of them, when you have finished adding and taking away the like terms you are left with nothing at all, so the answer is zero.

PROBLEM SOLVING

This is not a topic like the others in the book, because this applies to all aspects of mathematics. What it is about is how to deal with complicated and difficult questions, usually ones that come in several sentences, rather than ones that just have numbers, and plus or minus signs.

Here are the basic rules for problem solving:

(1)   *Read the question carefully.*
Try to make sure you understand it. If you are not in an examination, and you do not understand the question, ask your teacher or someone else.

(2)   *Deal with each part of the question in turn.*
When questions come in more than one part, treat each part separately. The parts will usually be in the order that makes most sense for working out the answers. Very often the answer to the first part will lead on to the second part, and so on.

(3)   *Decide what sort of calculation is involved.*
The question as a group of words looks difficult. Once you decide what set of mathematical processes you need to employ, it may well become a lot easier. It may well just involve the four rules, or a mathematical formula which you know.

(4)   *Note down the key points of the question.*
This means take the numbers out of the words. Often a whole sentence can be reduced to a single key word followed by a number.

(5)   *Set out your working clearly.*
Sometimes (quite often in fact) marks are given for working as well as for the final answer. But the main reason for working clearly is that you will then know what you are doing. Lots of scribbled sums on scraps of paper lead to confusion and the wrong answer.

(6)   *Write your answer(s) clearly and label them as answers.*
Sometimes it is difficult to tell where the answer is among a mass of working out. Do not make this mistake, which can lose you marks in exams for no reason at all.

(7)   *Check that your answer makes sense.*
Many answers that people write down are obviously ridiculous. If you are asked how long ten men take to dig a hole, and your answer is ten million days, then you have got it wrong (unless the hole in question was a very very big one). Answers to questions set in exams are sometimes weird numbers - but not very often. Bear that in mind, and check back.

(8)   *Quickly check your working.*
Even if your answer looks right, have a quick look at the working. If it looks wrong, look much more closely. Have you multiplied somewhere when you should have divided ? Have you missed out a decimal point or put it in the wrong place ?

Example (a)

A school organised a Sponsored Save for charity. The target was £48.00 pounds each, and five hundred and eighteen children each saved this sum.

(i)   How much did they save altogether ?   (ii)   How much short of £30,000 was this ?
(iii) If each of the children had saved sixty pounds, how much more than the first amount would the new overall total have been ?

(1)   *Read the question.* It is not that complicated - but it sounds as if it is. Don't panic ! Read it slowly, trying to understand what it is saying.

(2)   *Deal with each part in turn.* Here the three parts follow each other in the logical order. So start with the first. (Unless you have a very good reason, always start with the first.)

So we are now dealing with part (i) only.

(3)   *Decide what sort of calculation is involved.* Think about it. They saved £48.00 pounds each. You need to know how much all 518 saved. It sounds like multiplication.

(4)   *Note down the key points of the question.* We don't need all that stuff about a sponsored save. All we need is the numbers and the key words:

    Children -   518
    Saved -   £48.00
    Total saved - 518 x £48.00

(5)   *Set out your working clearly.*
    Like this:

$$
\begin{array}{r}
5\ \ 1\ \ 8 \\
\times\ \ \ \ 4\ \ 8 \\
\hline
4\ \ 1\ \ 4\ \ 4 \\
2\ \ 0\ \ 7\ \ 2\ \ 0 \\
\hline
2\ \ 4\ \ 8\ \ 6\ \ 4 \\
\hline
\end{array}
$$

(6)   *Write your answers clearly and label them as answers:*

    (i)   <u>Answer: They saved £ 24 864 altogether.</u>

(7)   *Check that your answer makes sense.* Well, it seems an awful lot of money, but then think about it. There were over five hundred children, and they raised nearly fifty pounds each. 500 x 50 = 25 000. So we are obviously in the right sort of area. Suppose you had made a silly mistake, and divided 518 by 48. Your result would be £10.7916666666 etc. Firstly this looks like nonsense. Secondly, if you think about it, it has to be wrong. It means that 518 children saved a smaller sum than one child.

(8)   *Quickly check your working.* Make sure that you have not made any silly mistakes in the multiplication, or forgotten to add any of the figures you carried.

We now move on to part (ii). It is sensible to reread the question at this point.

(3)   *Decide what sort of calculation is involved.* You have now worked out how much they actually did save altogether. Here you are being asked how much that amount is short of £30,000. What is the difference between the two amounts ? That is simple subtraction.

(4)   *Note down the key points of the question.* Again all we need is the numbers and key words:
        Saved -   £24 864
        Possible -   £30 000
        Difference -   £30 000 - £24 864

(5)   *Set out your working clearly.* Like this:

£   3 $^{9\cancel{10}}\cancel{0}$ $^{9\cancel{10}}\cancel{0}$ $^{9\cancel{10}}\cancel{0}$ $^{1}0$
           2   4   8   6   4 -
        _____
           £   5   1   3   6
        _____

(6)   *Write your answers clearly and label them as answers:*

        (i)   Answer: This was £ 5 136 short of £ 30 000.

(7)   *Check that your answer makes sense.* It seems to make very obvious sense. If we had added the two figures we would have nearly £55 000 as the answer, which would make no sense at all.

(8)   *Quickly check your working.* In this sort of subtraction, where you have a lot of zeros on the top line it is well worth making sure you have not made a mistake in the borrowing and repaying process.

We now move on to part (iii). It is sensible to read the question yet a third time at this point.

(3)   *Decide what sort of calculation is involved.* It looks rather more complicated this time, and for the good reason that there are two calculations involved. Firstly it is talking about everyone saving sixty pounds. So you have another multiplication, to find out the new total. Then it asks for the difference between the old total and the new total - another subtraction.

(4)   *Note down the key points of the question.* Again all we need is the numbers and the key words:
        New total -   £60 x 518
        Old total -   £24 864
        Difference -   New total - £24 864

(5)   *Set out your working clearly.* This time there are two stages of working. First a multiplication:

               5   1   8
        x   6   0
        _____
        3   1   0   8   0
        _____
               1   4

134

The second piece of working is a subtraction:

$$\begin{array}{cccccc} £ & 3 & {}^{10}\cancel{4} & {}^{1}0 & {}^{7}\cancel{8} & {}^{1}0 \\ & 2 & 4 & 8 & 6 & 4 & - \\ \hline & & 6 & 2 & 1 & 6 \\ \hline \end{array}$$

(6)   *Write your answers clearly and label them as answers:*

    (i)   <u>Answer: The new total would have been £ 6 216 more than the original total.</u>

(7)   *Check that your answer makes sense.* Once again, it seems to make good sense.

(8)   *Quickly check your working.* This time you have two calculations to check. In a multiplication it is always worth making sure you inserted any necessary zeros.

Normally that would be the end of the process, but there is an important point to be made here. In part (iii) we have arrived at the correct answer, but there was in fact a simpler way of doing it.

We could have said: *How much more does **each** child save ?*
We have another subtraction.
The £60 now stated minus the £48 actually collected: £ 60 - £ 48 = £ 12.
So if each child saves an extra £12, the total extra saved will be:
$$518 \text{ (the number of children) } \times 12 \text{ (the amount).}$$
If you work out this multiplication, you will come to the same result: £ 6 216.

The point is that this is easier. We still had to do a multiplication, but the subtraction was a simple piece of mental arithmetic, with no risk of mistakes in it.

Always look out for short-cuts. There is often a simple way of doing things, and the figures used in questions are often specifically chosen so that there is an easy way and a hard way. One good example is in the case of calculations involving fractions. Always watch out for possibilities of cancelling. There will nearly always be at least one pair of numbers that can be cancelled, thus making the calculation substantially easier.

On the following page there is a special ***Problems Practice***. This is like an exercise, and you have to try and work out the answers. The difference is that you are given help and advice, to make things clearer, and get you used to doing problems.

Problems Practice

For each problem, try to approach it using the eight steps given you on page 121.
In each case there is advice on how to handle the particular question.

1.   Fred and Mary go on a hiking holiday together for 45 days. In the course of the holiday
      they spend an average of £6.78 per day throughout the 45 day holiday. They draw all the
      money they spend from their joint account which contains, at the start, a total of £1 000.
      (a)   How much do they spend altogether during their holiday ?
      (b)   How much is left in their account at the end ?

*You have to sort out the information required, and what you must do with it. For part (a) the question
is how much altogether. You know how much for one day and the total number of days. So it is daily
amount times the number of days.*
*For part (b) you need the information you have just worked out - the total spent, and the amount you
are told they had to start with. What did they have left ? - The original total minus what they spent.*

2.   Four friends contribute money to a charitable organization in the ratio: 2 : 4 : 5 : 7.
      If the largest amount contributed is £1.40, calculate the total contribution of all four people.

This is a good opportunity to revise Topic 17 - Ratio, *on page 86. You should see that the way to
get to the answer is add the four ratios to get a total - 18 in this case. The separate rations then
become fractions of this total - eighteenths. You know that the largest fraction, seven eighteenths,
is £1.40. So one eighteenth is £1.40 divided by seven. You know one eighteenth, how do you find
eighteen eighteenths ?*

3.   What is the nearest number over five thousand which can be divided exactly by 61.

*Start by dividing 5 000 by 61. What you will get is 81, remainder 59. That means it very very nearly
went 82 times. How many more would you need to make it go 82 times. How many do you need to
make 59 into 61 ? That is the number you need to add to 5 000.*

4.   A path 500 m. long and 2 m. wide is to be made of concrete 25 cm. thick. Find:
      (a)   The quantity in cubic metres of concrete required.
      (b)   The cost of concreting the path at £33.57 per cubic metre.

*As usual with two part questions, you need to get the first part worked out in order to be able to do the
second. If you were not sure that this question was about volume, the mention of the word cubic in the
question should have told you instantly.*
Check Topic 12 - Volume *on page 66. You will find that you need to multiply the three measurements
together to find the volume of the concrete. To do this they all need to be in the same measurement.
25 cm. is a quarter of a metre, so you could do it in metres:*
$500 \times 20 \times {}^1\!/_4 = ?$ *cu. m.   You can work that one out. (Consider that multiplying by a quarter
is the same as dividing by 4. This is the sort of short cut you need to look out for.)*
*Now you know the amount of concrete needed in cubic metres, you need to multiply the figure by the
cost per cubic metre to answer part (b). Be careful - it is always easy to make mistakes in long
multiplication of decimals. Glance at the examples on page 20 if you have forgotten the method.*

5.	A total of 5 548 people went on the boat trip to Elston's Paradise Villa in the course of one summer season. Each boat load consisted of exactly thirty eight people, and the boat only sailed when it was full to capacity. The cost of one sailing is £44.00 per boat load inclusive.

(a)	How many sailings were there altogether ?

(b)	What was the total cost ?

For part (a), you know how many people go on one sailing (38), and you know that the grand total of people who sailed was 5 548. What do you do with these two numbers to find how many sailings ? This is a good example of getting nonsense as your result if you do the wrong thing with them ! For part (b), you have now worked out how many sailings there were. You are given the cost of one sailing. So again you have two numbers, and need to decide what calculation to perform with them. Again, if you do the wrong thing, your answer should look wrong.

6.	A room measures 16 m. by 24 m. It has a rectangular carpet in the middle, around which there is a continuous border 2 m. wide. Calculate the following:

(a)	the perimeter of the room		(b)	the perimeter of the carpet

(c)	the area of the room		(d)	the area of the carpet

(e)	the area of the border between the carpet and the walls

(f)	the total cost of the carpet at £14.76 per square metre.

In questions involving area and perimeter, it sometimes helps to draw a diagram. See if you can do one for this particular questions, and write the measurements you are given on it.

Perimeter is in Topic 10 *on page 60, and area in* Topic 11 *on page 63. If you want to check them, do so first. In fact, however, the formulas you need to use are very simple.*

Area is length times width.

Perimeter is twice (length plus width).

This is not the problem. The problem is sorting out the border. Look at your diagram. The carpet is two metres in from the wall all the way round. So it is two metres shorter at one end - and two metres shorter at the other end. It is two metres less wide at one end, and two metres less wide at the other end. This is the trick in the question. The carpet is not 24 minus 2 metres long; it is 24 minus 4 metres long; and 16 minus 4 metres wide.

You can now work out the area and perimeter of the carpet as well as those of the room. To find the area of the border - simply subtract carpet area from room area.

As for the price, you have found the area in square metres of the carpet, and you know the price of one square metre. What calculation do you have to perform ?

TESTS

The tests on the following pages are divided into three sections:

(a)   Mental arithmetic

These are questions involving calculations which should be done in the head, with a few jottings on paper allowed as the only working. The questions may be given from the book, or verbally. A time limit should normally be imposed for the whole test of a maximum of fifteen minutes. They include some in problem form and are designed to test reasoning ability as well as basic knowledge of key mathematical facts.

(b)   Calculations

The calculations in these tests are based on the four rules and their application to various measures and quantities. The questions are presented as pieces of straightforward arithmetic, and are designed to test and practice skills of computation. Part of these skills is the ability to set out the calculations in the proper form, and to show working neatly and efficiently. If a time limit is set, thirty to forty five minutes should be sufficient for most pupils, though a longer time would be appropriate for younger or less able children.

(c)   Problems

The problems are verbal formulations involving the application of the same basic mathematical skills. They are primarily designed to test reasoning skills, and the ability to apply knowledge of mathematics to practical examples, and to understand which skills and operations are required to deal with specific problems. An hour to an hour and thirty minutes would be an appropriate time limit for these tests.

Twelve tests have been provided in each section, and each test covers a selection from the range of skills taught within this book. The tests may be used specifically as timed tests, or as supplementary practice exercises without a time limit.

Test 1

1. Take $^1/_2$ from $1^1/_2$.
2. Write in figures the number which is two less than one hundred thousand.
3. What number when multiplied by 8 gives the answer 56 ?
4. How many grams are there in $^3/_4$ kg. ?
5. What is the total number of metres equal to $3\,^1/_4$ km. ?
6. How many minutes are there from a quarter to three to twenty five past three a.m. ?
7. If an express train travels at 150 kilometres per hour, how long will it take to travel 300 km. ?
8. Find the cost of 100 pencils at 12p. each.
9. What is the total cost of eight pairs of socks at £1.50 per pair ?
10. A gang of workers lay 30 metres of roadway every six days. How long will it take them to lay 120 metres of roadway working at the same rate ?

Test 2

1. 7030 ÷ 100
2. How many 20p. coins are there in £5.60 ?
3. 63 + 18 + 7
4. Write down all the factors of 36.
5. Which three coins are given in change after spending £3.75 from a five pound note ?
6. If one article costs £1.20, what will eight such articles cost ?
7. By how many grams is the total of 727 and 173 grams less than two kilograms ?
8. Class One has 25 children. Class two has 20 children. Class Three has 30 children. What is the average number of children per class ?
9. How many minutes are there from 01.16 hours to 02.32 hours ?
10. Take three thousand and ten from 6 060.

Test 3

1. How many complete hundreds are there in 60 371 ?
2. Write down the first seven multiples of 8.
3. 3 litres minus 0.715 litres. Answer in millilitres.
4. How many sixths are there in seven whole ones ?
5. What number is $^3/_4$ of 200 ?
6. Subtract $^3/_4$ of 200 from $^1/_5$ of 2 000.
7. What number is 639 less than 3 000 ?
8. Write these numbers in order of size, largest first: 63   7 374   286   3 944   818.
9. What is the cost of 11 articles at 99 pence each ?
10. Fill in the missing digit in the following fractions: $^3/_8 = ^?/_{64}$

Test 4

1. _____ + £ 2.24 = £ 6.00.
2. 11 sweets cost 70p. How much will 55 sweets cost ?
3. How many grams in $4\,^1/_5$ kg. ?
4. Find the difference between 718 and 9 200.
5. A clock shows 09.31, but it is forty minutes fast. What is the correct time ?
6. Find the volume of a cube of side 4 m.
7. A cube has a base area of 9 m^2 . What is its volume ?
8. What fraction of a kilogram is 125 grams ?
9. Write 125 % as a mixed number.
10. How far will a cyclist travel in $5\,^1/_2$ hours at a speed of 12 km. per hour ?

Test 5

1. How many days and hours are there in 77 hours ?
2. What is the product of 713 and 6 ?
3. Decrease $7\,^1/_2$ m. by 250 cm.
4. Write these fractions in order of size, largest first: $^9/_{10}$ $^1/_2$ $^1/_4$ $^3/_4$ $^2/_3$
5. 7 m. 73 cm. = ? mm.
6. 370 + 40 + 526
7. What is the nearest number to seventy into which six divides exactly ?
8. Write down the largest possible number which you can make using the digits: 0 3 8 6 7 .
   Each digit may be used once only.
9. 10 litres of a drink cost £14.00. How much does 500 ml. cost ?
10. What is the lowest common multiple of: 3 4 and 5 ?

Test 6

1. Write 7 kg. 47 g. in grams.
2. Complete this series: 7   2   9   4   11   6   13   ....
3. Find 30% of £12.00.
4. What is the decimal equivalent of three quarters ?
5. Find 75 % of 16 kg.
6. 1000 articles cost £190 . How much does one article cost ?
7. Find the product of 7.5 and 8.
8. What is the value of the figure shown in heavy type in this number; 3 716 283 .
9. Approximate 487 167 to the nearest ten thousand.
10. If a bus travels at an average speed of a kilometre a minute, how far does it travel in an hour ?

Section (a)   Mental Arithmetic

Test 7

1. Find the sum of 6 300, 71 and 964.
2. Subtract 201 from the sum of 407 and 65.
3. What are the first three multiples of 21 ?
4. Jack ran at an average speed of $7\frac{1}{2}$ km/h. for three hours. How far had he run ?
5. How would you write $^{16}/_{25}$ as a percentage ?
6. $^{3}/_{5} + ^{1}/_{2}$
7. What are the factors of 27 ?
8. Subtract £ 2 135 from £ 6 000.
9. Share £110.00 in the ratio 2 : 5 : 4 .
10. A room four metres wide, is twice as long as its width. What is its area ?

Test 8

1. Approximate 3 715 267 to the nearest hundred.
2. Write in figures: forty-two million, nine thousand and sixteen.
3. Reduce the product of 12 and 30 by 160.
4. Divide $^{3}/_{7}$ by 3.
5. If a 450 ml. can of drink costs 65 p., what will you have to spend to by 1 800 ml. ?
6. What is the average of these four numbers: 26, 43, 13 and 18 ?
7. What is the perimeter of a lawn measuring 3.5 metres by 5 metres ?
8. Subtract the number of degrees in a right angle from the number of degrees in a full circle.
9. It takes three people twelve hours to build a wall. How long would it take twelve people to build the same wall working at the same rate ?
10. What is the highest common factor of 36 and 84 ?

Test 9

1. How many hours are there in one week ?
2. (12 x 12) + (11 x 11)
3. Round off 166 289 716 to the nearest thousand.
4. 191.6 - 27.81
5. A clock is 28 minutes fast. If the clock says the time is 16.13, what is the real time, in the *twelve* hour clock ?
6. What are the factors of 100 ?
7. Write down all the elements of the set: prime numbers between ten and twenty.
8. £3 000 was shared between two people in the ratio: 6 : 9. How much did each person get ?
9. If you give a ten pound note for a bill of £ 6.75, what is the least number of coins that you can receive as your change ?
10. If 14 articles cost £2.80, what would 30 of the same articles cost ?

141

Section (a)   Mental Arithmetic

The final three tests, on this page, are harder, and a longer time may be needed to complete them.

Test 10

1.   17 kg. is reduced by 60 %. How much is left ?
2.   Seven children saved £45 each. How much less than £ 1 000 was the total of their savings ?
3.   £ 50.64 was shared equally among eight children. How much did each child receive ?
4.   Peter ran at an average speed of 8 $\frac{1}{2}$ km/h. for five hours. How far short of running 50 km. was he at the end of the time ?
5.   Seventeen workers make 680 toys in one hour. How many could eleven people make in an hour, working at the same rate ?
6.   What is the aggregate of: 173, 290 and 6 478 ?
7.   Reduce the sum of 71 216 and 3 040 by 450.
8. $\frac{1}{10}$ of a school of 640 children are suffering with 'flu. How many children do not have 'flu ?
9. $\frac{5}{6}$ - $\frac{1}{4}$
10.   What is the total mass (= weight) of 100 tins each weighing 270 g. ? Answer in kilograms.

Test 11

1.   Write down the number that is 2 700 more than 7 301.
2.   Which of the following numbers is nearest to 10 000 ?
      9 996   1 001   10 002   9 099   10 010
3.   What is the least number of coins required to be given in change from a £20 note for items costing £ 18.49 in total ?
4.   What time will it be seven and three quarter hours after 11.20 p.m. ?
5.   What are the first four multiples of 36 ?
6.   Write the following in order of size, starting with the smallest: 0.601   0.106   0.610   0.160
7.   Subtract 80.08 from 137.6 .
8.   How long will it take to travel 300 km. at an average speed of 40 km/h. ?
9.   In a week a class of 22 children saved a total of £ 110. What is the average saving per child ?
10.   Complete the final two numbers in this series: $\frac{1}{2}$ 15 $\frac{3}{4}$ 25   1   35   __   __ .

Test 12

1.   180 + 27 + 601 - 700
2.   Find the product of 807 and 12.
3.   Write 6 m. 17 cm. as millimetres.
4.   Which is larger: 80 % of £ 6 000, or 40 % of £ 8 000 ?
5.   What are the prime factors of 76 ?
6.   (68 ÷ 17) x (0.79 + 1.21)
7.   Tom had half as much as Sid. Sid had a quarter as much as Jack. If there was £8.80 to be shared, how much did each boy get ?
8.   Twelve people on the production line take five hours to complete a car. How long would twenty people working at the same rate take to complete ten cars ?
9.   A bus leaves at 3.30, and arrives, 150 km. away, at 5.00. What is its average speed ?
10.   Three articles cost £12.00 each, Four articles cost £16.00 each. What is the average cost ?

Test 1

1.   603 + 78 + 296   2.   871 - 396   3.   795 x 8

4.   8955 ÷ 5   5.   £ 62.38 x 26   6.   701.7 kg - 39 kg. 926 g.

7.   17 hr. 57 min. + 14 hr. 38 min. + 6 hr. 29 min.   8.   4921 ÷ 35

9.   6 days 21 hr. - 3 days 22 hrs.   10.   2 litres 625 ml. - 1.875 litres

Test 2

1.   589 + 978 + 2362   2.   1 696 - 975   3.   £ 79.6 x 7

4.   £ 56.49 ÷ 7   5.   76.59 x 37   6.   25 kg. 275g - 8.758 kg.

7.   25 % of 296   8.   0.739 + 13.64 + 270. 8002

9.   74.610 ÷ 90   10. $\frac{4}{5} + \frac{2}{3}$

Test 3

1. $\frac{7}{8} - \frac{1}{4}$ 2. $\frac{3}{5} \times \frac{4}{9}$ 3. $2\frac{5}{9} + 1\frac{2}{3}$

4. $2\frac{5}{9} \div 1\frac{2}{3}$ 5.   35.27 x 18   6.   256.64 kg ÷ 16

7.   125 % of £164.60   8.   52 km. 570 m. x 19   9.   24605 ÷ 35

10.   11.30 m. + 249 cm. + 7680 mm.

Test 4

1.   12 696 - 2 798   2.   1 888 ÷ 8   3.   278.98 ÷ 1.3

4.   1 272 m. 595 mm + 3 km. 928 m. 28 cm. 3 mm.   5.   204.01 x 0.38

6. $1\frac{11}{12} \times 3\frac{3}{23}$ 7.   Find the area of a square of side 27.3 cm.

8. $5\frac{5}{8} \div 6\frac{1}{4}$ 9.   44.394 kg ÷ 14   10. $7\frac{1}{6} - 6\frac{7}{8}$

Section (b)   Calculations

Test 5

1.   £ 982.63 + 12 387 pence   2.   79.86 - 2.374   3.   £14.72 x 2.5

4.   16 hours 18 minutes 21 seconds   minus 5 hours   29 minutes   36 seconds.

5.   What is the ratio of 300 metres to 1 kilometre ?   6.   38.754 ÷ 0.18

7.   What is the volume of a cube of side 12 mm. ?   8. $87\frac{1}{2}$ % of 88

9.   What is the perimeter of rectangle 13.5 metres long and 8.2 metres wide ?

10.   What is the volume of a cuboid measuring 3 cm. by 4 cm. by 5 cm. ?

Test 6

1.   Add 0.32, 3.02, 32 and 30.02   2.   Subtract 82.17 from 100.06

3.   Divide 319.804 litres by 3.4   4.   Multiply 0.019 metres by 293.

5.   What is 15 percent of £120.40 ?   6.   What is the ratio of 500 m. to 2 km. ?

7.   What is the L.C.M. of 8 and 12 ?   8.   What is the H.C.F. of 108 and 90 ?

9.   Add $3\frac{7}{16}$ to $5\frac{3}{4}$ 10.   Subtract $3\frac{5}{6}$ from $4\frac{1}{8}$

Test 7

1.   257.67 ÷ 0.09   2.   65.803 x 3.05   3.   140 % of £110.55

4.   52.375 km. + 976 m.   5.   8 h. 29 min. 16 sec. - 7 h. 52 min. 47 sec.

6. $3\frac{7}{9}$ ÷ $1\frac{5}{12}$ 7.   How many minutes are there in three days ?

8. $1\frac{3}{5}$ x $3\frac{1}{8}$ 9.   What are the prime factors of 66 ?

10.   Divide he sum of 28 h. 45 min. 32 sec. and   19 h. 24 min. 22 sec. by 13.

Test 8

1.   7.98 litres x 0.51. (Answer in millilitres.)   2.   £ 543.74 ÷ 31

3.   What is the area of a square of side 46.57 cm. ?   4.   7 days 20 h. - 3 days 23 h.

5.   450 % of 860 grams. (Answer in kilograms.)   6.   Reduce $\frac{280}{315}$ to its lowest terms.

7. $\frac{31}{38}$ ÷ $\frac{17}{19}$ 8. $2\frac{22}{39}$ x $\frac{117}{121}$

9.   What is the average of 19, 23 and 18 ?   10.   Reduce 144 : 24 to its lowest terms.

Section (b)   Calculations

Test 9

1.   Convert 37.932 metres into centimetres.
2.   Convert 0.375 into a percentage.
3.   How many times does 12.5 go into 125 000 ?
4. $^{12}/_{15}$ of £ 75.00
5.   How many cubic centimetres are there 12.53 litres of water ?
6.   What is the perimeter of a square of side 3.79 metres ?
7.   What is the area of a rectangle 2.3 metres long and 43 cm. wide ?
8.   What is the volume of a rectangular box 5 mm wide, 1 cm. high, and 1.5 cm. long ?
9.   What is the average of: 16 km., 19 km., 15 km. and 21 km. ?
10. What percentage of 2 km. is 250 metres ?

Test 10

1.   0.375 metres + 1 m. 15 cm. + 240 mm.
2.   2 litres 132 ml. - 1 litre 794 ml.
3.   10 m. 94 cm. 8 mm. ÷ 238
4.   173.62 kg. x 1.7
5. $3^{8}/_{9} + {}^{5}/_{6} + 1^{2}/_{3}$
6    $2^{4}/_{11}$ x $3^{5}/_{13}$
7. $3^{7}/_{9} \div 1^{24}/_{27}$
8. $6^{5}/_{8} - 5^{11}/_{12}$
9.   How many minutes from 03.15 to 07.21 ?
10. What is the L.C.M. of 3 and 17 ?

Test 11

1.   What is the L.C.M. of 19 and 4 ?
2.   What is the ratio of 3 mm to 3 m. ?
3.   Find 101 % of 10.1 kg.
4.   What is the H.C.F. of 12 and 8 ?
5.   0.625 of £780
6.   Express $^{513}/_{117}$ in it simplest terms
7. $4^{4}/_{5} - 3^{5}/_{6}$
8. $3^{7}/_{15} \div 6^{2}/_{5}$
9. $^{13}/_{27}$ x $1^{1}/_{26}$
10. $2^{6}/_{7} + {}^{13}/_{14} + 8^{14}/_{28}$

Test 12

1.   (2.205 kg. + 795 g.) x 0.01
2.   (£343.67 - £78.39) ÷ 0.08
3. $(4^{4}/_{5} - 3^{5}/_{6})$ x $5^{5}/_{9}$
4. $(8^{1}/_{4} - 5^{7}/_{10}) \div 5^{3}/_{5}$
5.   How many minutes are there between 11.46 a.m. and 1.12 p.m. ?
6.   How far does a train travelling at 150 km/h. travel in 3.5 hours ?
7.   Find the average of: 7.9, 8.6, 5.4 and 10.1.
8.   If the volume of a cube is 27 cubic centimetres, what is the length of its side ?
9.   If the perimeter of a square is 125 mm., what is the length of its side ?
10. If, in a universal set there are two sets only, each of three elements, with an intersection of two elements, how many elements are in the universal set ?

SECTION (C)   PROBLEM SOLVING

Test 1

1.   If it takes 14 men six weeks to mend the road, how long should it take 21 men to do the same job working at the same rate ?

2.   What is the total cost of fifty school ties at £3.46 each ?

3.   Give the total weight in kilograms of sixty four packets of cereal, each weighing 250 grams.

4.   A man lost £ 1 295 when he sold a car that had cost him £4 900. What did he sell it for ?

5.   The product of two numbers is 4 800. If one of the numbers is 32, what is the other number ?

6.   How many bags each containing $2^1/_4$ kg. of sugar can be filled from a full 550 kg. box of sugar ?

7.   Find the cost of a gross (1 gross = 144) of eggs at £1.80 per dozen.

8.   From the sum of: twenty-six million and two; four hundred thousand and ninety-eight; and nine hundred and ninety five; subtract the product of 204 and 15 647.

9.   Reduce the difference between 892.06 and 587.57 by the dividend of 472.68 and 9.09 .

10.   In a school of 465 children, $^3/_5$ are girls. How many boys are there in the school ?

Test 2

1.   I bought a clock in a sale, and then sold it on to another person for £ 293.75. In doing so I made a profit of £18.93. What was the price I originally paid for the clock ?

2.   How many hours are there altogether in the last two months of the year ?

3.   At a concert attended by 540 men and women, $^4/_9$ of the audience were men. How many women attended ?

4.   How many times can $^1/_5$ be subtracted from 12.2 ?

5.   A bunch of eight carnations costs £ 1.50. How much would you have to pay for 96 carnations ?

6.   A cyclist cycles at an average speed of 18 km/h. How long will it take him to cycle 12 km. ?

7.   (a)   How many 45 cm. lengths of wire can be cut from a reel of wire 11 metres long ?
        (b)   What length of wire is there left ?

8.   In respect of the sum of £ 9.45:
        (a)   How many five pence coins make up this sum ?
        (b)   What is the smallest possible number of coins and notes (excluding £2.00 coins) which could make up this sum ?
        (c)   How many articles priced at 22 pence each could I buy for this sum ?

9.   An athlete running in a 1 500 metres race dropped out 276 metres from the finishing line. His time for the distance he had completed was five minutes and six seconds exactly.
        (a)   How far had the athlete run
        (b)   What was his speed in metres per second ?
        (c)   What was his speed in kilometres per hour ?
        (d)   If he had completed the race at the same speed, what would his finishing time have been ?

10.   Two thirds of the children in a school play cricket. A quarter of the remaining children in the school do swimming. If there are 600 children altogether in the school, how many do not take part in either activity ?

146

Section (c) Problem Solving

Test 3

1. If a man's stride measures exactly 90 cm., how many strides will he take to walk 1 080 metres ?

2. Find the cost of 157 newspapers at 32 p. each.

3. When 17 is multiplied by another number the product is 54 604. What is the other number ?

4. How many 250 ml. bottles can be filled from a 2 500 litre tank ?

5. Add 0.75 to $^1/_3$ of $4^1/_2$. Give your answer as a decimal number.

6. How long will it take a car travelling at an average speed of 90 km/h. to travel 108 km. ?

7. Five litres of petrol cost £ 3.65. How many litres could you buy for £ 64.97 ?

8. If twelve men lay 60 m. of pavement in 9 days, how long will it take six men, working at the same rate, to lay 120 m. of pavement ?

9. Find the average height in *metres* of four boys measuring: 149, 151, 146 and 164 *centimetres*.

10. In a team of 15 players there are 7 more boys than girls. How many girls are in the team ?

Test 4

1. Divide the product of ninety-thousand and ninety and one hundred and fifty-seven by 900.

2. There are 960 passengers in a train of 15 coaches.
    (a)   What is the average number of passengers in each coach ?
    (b)   At Crewe three coaches are removed from the train, 139 passengers get off, and 19 passengers get on.   What is the new average of passengers per coach ?

3. A tin of fruit weighs 470 g.
    (a)   What would be the weight of a pack of 1 200 tins of fruit ?
    (b)   How much would such a pack cost at the wholesale price of 13.5 p. per dozen tins ?

4. A boy weighs 4.99 kg. more than his sister. If he weighs 43.625 kg., what is his sister's weight ?

5. What is the ratio of boys to girls in a school of 636 pupils where 412 of them are girls ?

6. It takes the paper-girl on average one and a half hours to deliver seventy-five newspapers. How long would it take six girls to deliver 450 papers working at the same rate ?

7. Add 25 % of 2.5 tonnes to 0.75 of 2 500 000 grams. Answer in kilograms.

8. Subtract the sum of the prime factors of 34 from the difference between the H.C.F. of 72 and 96 and the L.C.M. of 8 and 9.

9. Two ferries leave Harwich in the evening. Ferry A to the Hook of Holland leaves at 10.30 and arrives at 6.30 a.m. on the following day, after a journey of 200 km. Ferry B leaves at 11.20, and arrives at Zeebrugge at 5.20 a.m. after a journey of 150 km. Which ferry is faster ?

10. In a wall measuring 12.25 metres long by 3.5 metres high, there are three square windows each window has an area of 1.69 m^2.
    (a)   What is the area of the wall excluding the windows ?
    (b)   What is the height of each window ?
    (c)   What is the total outside perimeter of the wall ?

Test 5

1.   A bus has seats for 54 passengers. How many seats do 54 buses have ?

2.   A man is paid 5 % interest in cash on an investment of £ 3 000 every year for five years. How much cash in total does he receive as interest over the five years ?

3.   If I spend £ 56.00 buying seven meals, what will I have to spend to buy 13 at the same price ?

4.   The area of a playground is 960 m^3 . If its length is 60 m. what are its width and perimeter ?

5.   In the course of a month a woman makes four weekly payments each of £ 113.46 into her bank account. She withdraws two amounts: £ 98.35 and £ 217.64. Her balance at the beginning of the month was £ 1 235.41. What is her balance at the end of the month ?

6.   How many square metres of wood are needed to make a table top 5 m. long and 3 m. wide ?

7.   From one and five eighths subtract the result of dividing one and three fifths by six and four tenths.

8.   28 campers have enough food for 42 days. Another 21 campers join them (at the start before any food is used), and they all have to share the same food. How long will the food now last ?

9.   A jug has a volume of 400 cm^3 . What percentage of a litre of water can it hold ?

10.   If I earn £ 115 for six hours work, what will I earn in a 36 hour working week ?

Test 6

1.   A swimming pool is $8\frac{1}{2}$ metres wide. How far does a boy swim when he swims 19 widths ?

2.   What is the weight in kilograms of 93 parcels each weighing 807 grams ?

3.   A girl read $\frac{1}{8}$ of a book which was 104 pages long. It took her exactly twenty six minutes. If she reads at the same rate, how long will it take her to finish the book ?

4.   Find the difference between 0.375 of £ 12.00 and $\frac{3}{8}$ of £ 9.60.

5.   Alan saved 5 pence every day of the year, and Tony saved six pence every day of the year. How much more than Alan did Tony save ? (*It is not a Leap Year.*)

6.   What is the smallest number of coins you could receive in change from £100.00 after buying nine model cars priced at £ 9.56 each ? (*Do not include £2.00 coins.*)

7.   What is the lowest number which needs to be added to 871 to make it exactly divisible by 19 ?

8.   In an orchard, 50 % of all the trees are apple trees, $\frac{1}{6}$ are pear trees, and the rest are plum trees. If there are 30 plum trees, how many apple trees and pear trees are there ?

9.   Nicholas and David weigh a total of 146 kg. Nicholas weighs 4 kg. more than David. How much does each boy weigh ?

10.   A shrubbery is 18 m. long and 13 m. wide. All the way round it is a path three m. wide.
        (a)   What is the area of the path ?
        (b)   What is the outer perimeter of the path ?
        (c)   What is the inner perimeter of the path ?

Section (c)   Problem Solving

Test 7

1.   Find the cost of 15 % if the cost of 50 % is £10.00

2.   A train leaves Birmingham at 9.45 a.m. and arrives in Glasgow at 4.28 p.m., a journey of 403 km.
      (a)   How long did the journey take ?
      (b)   What was the average speed of the train ?

3.   Buns are sold at £1.32 per half dozen. How many could you buy for £18.48 ?

4.   How many packets of tea, each holding 125 grams can be filled from a chest holding 25 kg. ?

5.   If eight pens cost 63 p., what would be the cost of 96 pens ?

6.   A patient has to take five daily doses each consisting of one 5 ml. teaspoon of medicine.
      How many *complete* days will a bottle of medicine containing $2/_5$ of a litre last ?

7. $(2^1/_7 - 1^2/_3) \div {}^5/_? = {}^2/_3$. What is the missing digit ?

8.   If the difference between two numbers is two, and their sum is 12, what are the numbers ?

9.   Tom, Dick and Harry win a sum of money in a raffle, and divide it between themselves in the
      same ratio as the sums they paid towards the ticket. Tom contributed 12 p. towards the ticket,
      Dick contributed 8 p. towards it, and Harry contributed 10 p. Their winnings are £12.60.
      How much does each of them receive as his share ?

10.   A family's weekly bill consists of £ 76.85 for food, £ 9.02 for electricity, and £ 10.40 for gas,
      and £ 28.73 for mortgage repayments, with a further £ 25.00 allowed for clothes.
      (a)   How much money do they have to spare out of an income of £175.00 per week ?
      (b)   What *fraction* of their income goes on the weekly expenditure ?
      (c)   What *percentage* of their expenditure is allocated to clothes ?

Test 8

1.   If I pay income tax at the rate of 25 p. in the pound, what will I have left from my salary
      if I receive a total of £ 15 600 per annum ?

2.   How much money would 12 men earn in two days, if 32 men, who are paid at the same rate,
      earn £ 11 520 in 12 days ?

3.   Find the nearest number to 7 000 which is exactly divisible by 34.

4.   Increase the product of 3.92 and 0.5 by the difference between 3.029 and 5.263.

5.   Divide a steel rod measuring 12.65 metres in the ratio 2 : 5 : 4.

6.   If one man can do the work of two boys, how long would it take five men and two boys
      to do a piece of work that one man can do in twelve days ?

7. $(3^3/_4 + ?^7/_8) \div 4^4/_9 = 25$. What is the missing digit ?

8.   The average hourly wage of three workers is £5.40. If Sally earns £5.45 per hour, and
      Mandy earns £6.18 per hour, what does Annie earn per hour ?

9.   A cheetah can race at a kilometre a minute, and a rhino can charge at 50 000 metres an hour.
      Which would cover a distance of a third of a kilometre faster, and by how much ?

10.   How many litres of water would fill a pool measuring 25 m. by 15 m. by 7m. ?

Section (c) Problem Solving

Test 9

1. Twelve meals cost £156.00 altogether. What would seven meals cost at the same price ?

2. 35 men can erect a fence in 12 days. How long would it take 42 men working at the same rate ?

3. After eight innings a cricketer's average was 53 runs. After he had played another four innings, his average had risen to 77 runs. What was his average for the last four innings ?

4. Find the value of one kilogram of metal priced at £4 780 per tonne.

5. A box contains £ 55.00 in 2p., 5p. and 50p coins . If there are two hundred 5p. coins, and forty-eight 50p. coins, how many 2p. coins are there in the box ?

6. What number multiplied by 49 will give the same number as 21 multiplied by 14 ?

7. Expensive cloth is two and a half times the price of cheap cloth. If cheap cloth costs £2.60 per metre, how much will it cost to buy 12 metres of expensive cloth ?

8. A rectangular field measures 120 m. by 80 m. A fence is put round the field leaving space for two gates each 4 m. wide. What length of fencing was required ?

9. A man starts work at 7.30 a.m. and works until 5.30 p.m., with one hour fifteen minutes allowed every day for lunch. How long does he work in a five day week ?

10. A cube of side 8 cm. is cut from a block of wood 9 cm. by 10 cm. by 14 cm. What volume of wood is left after the cube is cut out ?

Test 10

1. Fifty sheets of card have a total thickness 40 mm. How thick would 8 sheets of card be ?

2. Five apples weigh four hundred grams. How many similar apples would weigh 72 kg. ?

3. A cricket square of area 900 m². is marked off in the middle of a field measuring 95 m. by 110 m. What is the area of the field excluding the cricket square ?

4. Cards measuring 200 mm. x 240 mm. cost £ 1.20 per packet. How much would twelve packets of cards measuring 160 mm. x 200 mm. cost if priced on the same basis ?

5. A clock is started at 10.30 a.m. on Friday. It gains three minutes every hour. What time will the clock actually show when it is really 11.10 a.m. on the following Tuesday ?

6. What is the area of a rectangle of perimeter 32 m. and width of 7 m. ?

7. A train travelling at an average speed of 128 km/h. takes four hours exactly to complete its journey. How long will it take to complete the same journey if, for one quarter of its route, the speed is reduced to 64 km/h. ?

8. In a group of 125 children, 45 did Latin, 95 did French, and 30 did both subjects. By means of a Venn diagram work out how many children did neither subject.

9. A rope 18 m. long is cut into eight pieces. There are four short pieces, all equal, and there are four long pieces, also all equal. The short pieces are half the length of the long pieces.
    (a) How long are the short pieces ?   (b) How long are the long pieces ?

10. A trader purchased a batch of 135 items priced at £12.90 each at a thirty percent discount. How much did he pay for the batch of items ?

Test 11   *(A minimum of two hours should be allowed to complete this test.)*

1.   John buys a packet of 36 foreign stamps to start his stamp collection. He collects twelve more stamps every week. How many weeks will it take for his collection to reach 216 stamps in all ?

2.   How many 8 mm^3 cubes can be packed into box measuring 150 mm. x 20 mm. x 12 mm., so that the box is $^3/_4$ full of the cubes.

3.   A lorry travels at an average speed of 60 km. per hour in the course of a journey of 1 393 km. If it sets off at 8.17 a.m. on Tuesday, at what time of what day does it arrive at its destination ?

4.   In a class three children were absent through illness, two children were away on holiday, and one child was playing truant. If twenty percent were absent, what was the full class size ?

5.   A cube has three sides coloured green, one side blue and two sides yellow.
If you throw the cube into the air a hundred times, how many times would you expect it to land with one of the green sides on top ?

6.   Seventeen cubic metres of sand weigh 68 000 kg.
      (a)   What is the weight of 2.5 m^3 of sand ?
      (b)   What volume of sand weighs 600 g. ?

7.   A shopkeeper purchased an article for £ 37.50.
      (a)   At what price must he sell it to make a profit of £3.75 ?
      (b)   What is his percentage profit at this selling price ?
      (c)   How much would he make if he sold 147 such articles at the same profit ?
      (d)   At what price would he need to sell each article to make a profit of 20 % ?

8.   A container is filled with orange squash. When the container is exactly half full, the total weight of container and squash is 650 g. When it is completely full the total weight of container and squash is 1 000 g.
      (a)   Find the weight of the empty container.
      (b)   Find the weight of the quantity of orange squash required to fill it.
      (c)   Find the total weight of container and squash when it is $^1/_5$ full.

9.   Find the total cost of the following items on a shopping list:
      Three quarters of a pound of cheese at £3.80 a pound
      30 eggs at £1.80 per dozen
      5 $^1/_2$ kg. potatoes at 38 p. per kg.
      125 grams of ham at £6.40 per kg.

10.   Three soccer teams in the league competition scored the following number of points:
      Leeds and Coventry together made 41;
      Southampton and Leeds together made 43;
      All three teams made a total of 56 points.
How many points did each team make ?

Test 12   The " PROBLEM KING " Test

(A minimum of three hours should be allowed to complete this test.)

1.   A grocer mixes 3 kg. of tea for which he paid £4.00 per 1 000 g. with 6 kg. of tea
      for which he paid 85 p. per 250 g., to make a blended tea to sell in his shop.
      (a)   At what price per 100 g. must he sell the blend simply to cover his costs ?
      (b)   At what price per 100 g. should he sell the blend in order to make a profit of 20 % ?
      (c)   He decides to sell the mixture at 45 p. per 100 g., but he only manages to sell
             7 kg. at that price, so he sells of the rest at 20 p. per 100 g. How much money does
             he receive in total for the sale of all nine kilograms ?

2.   Study the following diagrams, and answer the questions below:

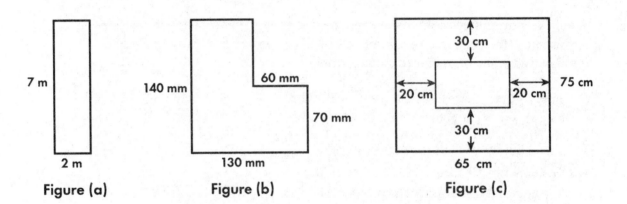

Figure (a)   Figure (b)   Figure (c)

      (a)   Calculate the area and perimeter of figure (a)
      (b)   Calculate the area and perimeter of figure (b)
      (c)   In figure (c), calculate the area and perimeter of the square inside the large rectangle.

3.   Draw a pie chart to show the use of time in a school day as follows:

Mathematics	1 hour
English	1 hour
Science	1 hour
History	30 minutes
Geography	30 minutes
P.E. and/or Games	1 hour
Lunch and Playtimes	1 hour 30 minutes
Assembly	30 minutes

      State what part of the day is spent on *lessons* as a fraction *and* as a percentage.

4.   A water tank measures 3 metres by one and a half metres by 50 centimetres.

      (a)   What is its capacity in litres ?
      (b)   What weight of water will it hold when completely filled ?
      (c)   The tank is filled from a tap which delivers water at a rate of 1 000 cubic centimetres
             every twenty seconds. How long will it take for the tap to fill the tank completely ?

test continued

5.   Using the following Venn diagram, answer the questions below.

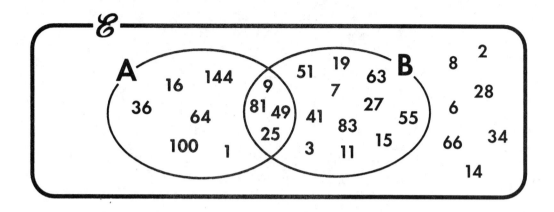

Write down (in the correct form, using the relevant symbols):

(a)   the elements of the universal set
(b)   the elements of Set A
(c)   the elements of Set B
(d)   the intersection of Set A and Set B
(e)   the union of Set A and Set B

(f)   Suggest a name for each of Sets A and B.

6.   Study the railway timetable you are given below and answer the questions which follow it.

Train number:-		1	2	3	4
Birmingham	*dep.*	06.50	07.55	09.56	10.45
Derby	*arr.*	07.36	08.38	10.36	11.23
Derby	*dep.*	07.38	08.43	10.37	11.24
York	*arr.*	9.10	10.55	12.00	13.25

(a)   What is the latest train I can catch from Birmingham to arrive at York by 11.00 a.m. ?
(b)   Which train takes the shortest, and which the longest time from Birmingham to York, and what is the difference between them in minutes ?
(c)   Which train takes stops for longest at Derby ? How long does it stop for ?
(d)   Calculate the average speed of train 3 only for the entire journey of 228 route kilometres between Birmingham and York.
(e)   What is the average journey time by train between Birmingham and York ?

test continued

7.   Look at this graph, and then answer the questions which follow it.

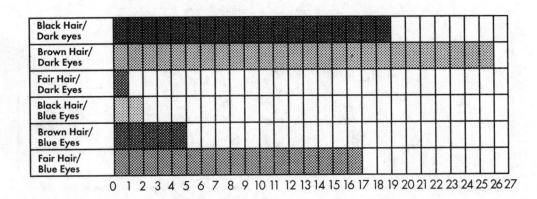

(a)   How many people were counted in the survey which produced these results ?

(b)   Which is the commonest combination of hair and eye colour, and by how many ?

(c)   Which two combinations are quite common and almost equal in numbers ?

(d)   Which combinations are rarest ?

(e)   By what other mathematical method might you show these combinations ?
        (*If you can think of more than one way, mention them.*)

8.   In a pack of fifty-two ordinary playing cards, well shuffled and randomly distributed, if a volunteer is asked to draw a card, and the card he draws is recorded. He repeats this process one thousand and forty times. How many times, according to mathematical probability, would you expect him to have drawn the ace of spades ?

9.   Three flashing lights mark the entrance to a harbour. The light on Stormy Point flashes every seven seconds. The light on Deadman's Cliff flashes every six seconds. The light in Fairway Channel flashes every four seconds. All three lights flash together at 12 . 00 .00 - exactly midday. What is the first time after midday when they will all flash together again ?

10.   Add the following:
        the sum of the angles of a triangle
        three right angles
        the number of degrees in a straight line
        a quarter of the angles in a rectangle.

        Give your answer in completed circles.